ENABLING TECHNOLOGY

DATE DUE

AP 20 04			

DEMCO 38-296

Disability, Human Rights and Society

Series Editor: Professor Len Barton, University of Sheffield

The *Disability, Human Rights and Society* series reflects a commitment to a particular view of 'disability' and a desire to make this view accessible to a wider audience. The series approach defines 'disability' as a form of oppression and identifies the ways in which disabled people are marginalized, restricted and experience discrimination. The fundamental issue is not one of an individual's inabilities or limitations, but rather a hostile and unadaptive society.

Authors in this series are united in the belief that the question of disability must be set within an equal opportunities framework. The series gives priority to the examination and critique of those factors that are unacceptable, offensive and in need of change. It also recognizes that any attempt to redirect resources in order to provide opportunities for discriminated people cannot pretend to be apolitical. Finally, it raises the urgent task of establishing links with other marginalized groups in an attempt to engage in a common struggle. The issue of disability needs to be given equal significance to those of race, gender and age in equal opportunities policies. This series provides support for such a task.

Anyone interested in contributing to the series is invited to approach the Series Editor at the Division of Education, University of Sheffield.

Current and forthcoming titles

M. Corker: *Deaf and Disabled, or Deafness Disabled?*
M. Moore, S. Beazley and J. Maelzer: *Researching Disability Issues*
A. Roulstone: *Enabling Technology: Disabled People, Work and New Technology*
C. Thomas: *Female Forms: Disabled Women in Social Context*
A. Vlachou: *Struggles for Inclusive Education: An Ethnographic Study*

ENABLING TECHNOLOGY
Disabled people, work and
new technology

Alan Roulstone

Open University Press
Buckingham · Philadelphia

MK18 1XW

email: enquiries@openup.co.uk
world wide web: http//www.openup.co.uk
and
325 Chestnut Street
Philadelphia, PA 19106, USA

First Published 1998

A catalogue record of this book is available from the British Library

ISBN   0 335 19801 5 (pb)   0 335 19802 3 (hb)

Library of Congress Cataloging-in-Publication Data
Roulstone, Alan, 1962–
    Enabling technology : disabled people, work, and new technology /
Alan Roulstone.
        p.   cm. — (Disability, human rights, and society)
    Includes bibliographical references and index.
    ISBN 0-335-19802-3. — ISBN 0-335-19801-5 (pbk.)
        1. Computers and the handicapped. 2. Computerized self-help devices for the
handicapped. 3. Handicapped—Employment. 4. Work environment—Access for
the physically handicapped. 5. Vocational rehabilitation. I. Title. II. Series.
HV1569.5.R69 1998
362.4'048—dc21   97-33099
                                                                        CIP

Copy-edited and typeset by The Running Head Limited, London and Cambridge
Printed in Great Britain by St Edmundsbury Press Ltd, Bury St Edmunds, Suffolk

Contents

Series editor's preface

The Disability, Human Rights and Society series reflects a commitment to a social model of disability and a desire to make this view accessible to a wide audience. 'Disability' is viewed as a form of oppression and the fundamental issue is not one of an individual's inabilities or limitations, but rather, a hostile and unadaptive society.

Priority is given to identifying and challenging those barriers to change, including the urgent task of establishing links with other marginalized groups and thus seeking to make connections between class, gender, race, age and disability factors.

The series aims to further establish disability as a serious topic of study, one in which the latest research findings and ideas can be seriously engaged with.

This book is an important and original contribution to a social barriers approach to the study of disabled peoples' experience of using new technology. Both the positive benefits and disabling aspects of the new technology developments are identified and discussed. A key insight which the book provides concerns the encouragement to view the connectedness, nature and function of disabling barriers.

Roulstone is critical of traditional rehabilitation models of technology benefits which he maintains view these issues in a social vacuum, support a deficit approach of disability by emphasizing the powerful benefits of the new technology to correct the disabled body and tend to provide a non-problematical approach to the impact of new technology on the working lives of disabled people.

Drawing on fieldwork including in-depth interviews of disabled people using new technology, the author provides some very illuminative insider accounts of the diverse routes by which disabled people come to be working with the new technology and the degree of significance it has played in their lives.

In exploring the extent to which new technology provides disabled people with an opportunity to develop a greater control of the employment environment as well as the potential it has for providing a basis for a redefinition of disability itself, Roulstone offers some thoughtful reflections on the complexity and subtlety of the factors involved in these questions.

He contends that this whole issue of new technology needs to be placed within a framework in which the configuration of existing barriers such as negative attitudes, disabling structures and the level of access to technology will be influential factors in determining the possibilities and limits of these developments and the establishment of this new topic as a rights issue.

Finally, the author draws out some important recommendations for new policy initiatives in the field of new technology and the employment of disabled people.

This is an important book on a very under-researched area and one which provides a wealth of ideas and points for discussion and further research. As such, it is essential reading for disabled and non-disabled people.

Professor Len Barton
Sheffield

Acknowledgements

This book would not have been possible but for the help, advice and patient endurance of a number of people. Special thanks go to Vic Finkelstein for his wisdom and guidance on the whole venture; thanks also to Len Barton for taking this work seriously; I hope my efforts repay your faith in this book. Thanks to Colin Barnes, Joanna Bornat, Geoff Busby, David Calderwood, Derek Childs, Cynthia Cockburn, Paul Cornes, Janis Firminger, Maggie Goodbarn, Susan Gregory, John Heppel, Mervyn Kettle, Derek Lambert, Peter Large, Helen McNally, Sheila Peace, Tom Shakespeare, Moyra Siddell, Tom Vincent, Adam Westoby and the late Irving Zola, who all contributed intellectually or materially to the book.

Gratitude also extends to Jacinta Evans and Joan Malherbe at the Open University Press for their support. Apologies and gratitude to Jo and Guy for putting up with my absenteeism during the completion of the book. In a work of this kind it is important to acknowledge the time and generosity of the disabled people who took part in the research: without them this book would not have been possible.

List of acronyms

ACT	Access to Technology
ADA	Americans with Disabilities Act
AEA	Access to Environments Act
AO	administrative officer
ATW	Access to Work
CCTV	closed circuit television
COBOL	Common Business-Oriented Language
CORAD	Committee on Restrictions against Disabled People
COSSH	Control of Substances Hazardous to Health
CP	cerebral palsy
CREST	Centre for Rehabilitation and Engineering Studies
DAS	Disablement Advisory Service
DDA	Disability Discrimination Act
DEA	disability employment adviser
DRO	disablement resettlement officer
EO	executive officer
IT	information technology
ME	myalgic encephalomyelitis
MS	multiple sclerosis
NACG	National Access Coordination Group
OPCS	Offices of Population, Censuses and Surveys
OU	Open University
PA	personal assistant
PACT	Placement Assessment and Counselling Team
PC	personal computer
RA	rheumatoid arthritis
RADAR	Royal Association for Disability and Rehabilitation
RNIB	Royal National Institute for the Blind
SAE	Special Aids to Employment

SCPR   Social and Community Planning Research
TAEA   Telecommunications Accessibility Enhancement Act
TIDE   Technology Initiative for Disabled and Elderly People
UMIST   University of Manchester Institute of Sciences and Technology
UPIAS   Union of Physically Impaired against Segregation
VDU   visual display unit

Introduction

This book, and the research on which it is based, is about disabled people, their lives and aspirations. Although the focus of the work is new technology and employment, the value of the findings rests in their illustration of the nature of social barriers and how they can be reduced. New technology, and its revolutionizing of much working life, is seen to hold particular benefits for disabled people. Access issues have begun to be redefined as alternative methods of working are made possible by microchip technologies.

The findings of this research are of great significance to many disabled people. They suggest that the advent of new technologies is helping to high-light and overcome diverse barriers. However, negative attitudes, disabling structures and technical problems continue to limit the extent of this redefinition of environments. The research identifies the *barriers* disabled people continue to face, and highlights the *configured* nature of the barriers – how they are connected and function.

The question, what is disability? is opened up for scrutiny when the use of enabling technology provides evidence of once-suppressed ability. These findings add significant weight to a social barriers model of disability which views social organization as the primary source of disability in contemporary society.

The book seeks to contribute to the growing body of literature which applies a social barriers model to the lives of disabled people. The policy focus of this work ensures that concrete policy solutions are offered. Here the importance of new technology in an enabling workplace suggests that technology policy should be framed alongside other access issues (transport, disabled parking, housing) as a rights issue. In this way, access to work and advancement should be viewed as a right where the disabled person is suitably qualified to perform a job, given the technological support required.

Only with a rights-based policy agenda will disabled people have the choice to use new technology to facilitate their access to paid work. A more voluntaristic approach and a simple remoulding of the current statutory scheme of aids and adaptations will mean that many disabled people continue to be denied access to the world of work. The fast-changing nature of employment and technical innovation makes it imperative that policy addresses the rights of disabled people if they are not to be further excluded from the employment domain.

Because of these changes we are faced with profound choices in terms of education, employment and leisure: new technology is going to be a pivotal factor in influencing and shaping these choices. Disabled people have a right to exploit fully the potential of new technology, to realize their abilities by casting off the fetters of a disabling society.

An overview of Part 1

This book is divided into three parts. Part 1 is a theoretical discussion of the wider issues in the study of new technology and its impact on the employment experiences of disabled people. By addressing a range of theoretical contributions from disability studies, rehabilitation writers, the sociology of employment, labour markets, and technology studies, Part 1 aims to:

- explore why new technology may a be particularly promising and enabling development for disabled workers and job seekers;
- examine critically different theoretical discourses which have been used to explain the promise and potential of new technology; and
- assess those factors likely to limit or facilitate the enabling use of new technology in disabled people's working lives.

Chapter 1 provides a theoretical discussion of the immense significance of new technology for disabled people in the contemporary workplace. It suggests that two very different models of disability can be applied to an understanding of this significance, and looks at how these models conceptualize the benefits of new technology for disabled people. A *social barriers* model is presented as the most useful and enabling model for understanding the value of new technology for disabled people; one which challenges established rehabilitation models of technology benefits, which can be termed a *deficit model* of technology benefits.

Chapter 2 looks at the changing nature of work and the spread of new technology into more areas of our working lives. The chapter explores the general promise of new technology and argues that the theoretical appraisal of this promise can be located within the broader discourse that surrounds the shift to a post-industrial society. The chapter argues that although this discourse accommodates both left and right political versions of the promise of post-industrialism, there are serious problems inherent in both perspectives. The quasi-evolutionary precepts that characterize aspects of this discourse obscure a number of specific historical, political, cultural and organizational factors which influence the extent to which this promise is realized.

Chapter 3 provides a review of research to date on the experiences of disabled workers using new technology. This chapter will illustrate how all previous research in this area has been informed by a deficit model of disability. It will be argued that this model views the benefits of new technology as inhering in its power to correct the disabled body. In this way the deficit model underplays the structural and attitude barriers that limit disabled people, and therefore overlooks the possibility that new technology may be most beneficial in correcting these disabling barriers.

Chapter 4 addresses directly the nature and likely extent of attitude and structural barriers. By looking at these barriers we can begin to predict the likely interplay between enabling technology and disabling environments. It is argued that pre-existing social structures are likely to shape the specific experiences of disabled people using new technology at work. Here, more general disabling attitudes and structures can be seen to be compounded by other structures of exclusion, for example sexism, racism and attitudes to specific impairments.

Chapter 5 explores the government-funded Special Aids to Employment scheme. In this chapter it is argued that as a measure providing specialized technological support for disabled workers, the scheme has held substantial enabling potential as a provider of technological aids where employers are unlikely, unwilling or only partially prepared to supply new technology. However, the scheme is portrayed as firmly embedded in a deficit model of disability, and its long history has created a cultural boundary around the provision of technological support and the discourse around the benefits of new technology. Such deficit assumptions have ensured that the scheme operates with little reference to disabled people's stated needs. As a policy intervention, the Special Aids to Employment scheme and its successor – now part of the Access to Work programme – have benefited few, while hampering discussion of a more enabling approach to new technology provision. This chapter is seen as central to this research in that the Special Aids to Employment scheme is the only substantial policy commitment to technology provision for disabled workers in the United Kingdom. This chapter will critically explore the premises and workings of the scheme and how they are linked.

An overview of Part 2

In Part 2 the reader is introduced to the core of the book: the empirical findings of national research which for the first time applies a social barriers model of disability to a detailed exploration of disabled people's employment experiences of new technology. The content of these chapters reflects the two-stage research methodology adopted for this study.

In Chapter 6 the findings of the first stage of the research are presented. Stage 1 took the form of a self-completion questionnaire despatched to a national sample of 78 disabled people. The questionnaire aimed to garner a broad national picture of disabled workers using new technology; this in turn would allow Stage 2 research to focus on a representative group of disabled people.

The second stage of the research took the form of in-depth semi-structured interviews with 30 disabled people. These participants were a representative sub-sample of the Stage 1 research group. This second stage aimed to draw out both the depth and nuances of experiences of enabling technology and those barriers which limited the enabling potential of new technology. Stage 2 findings were to provide qualitative ideas which it was hoped would triangulate with and support Stage 1 findings.

Chapter 7 begins the process of unpacking the qualitative findings to come out of Stage 2 of this study and looks at the diverse routes by which disabled people came to be working with new technology. This provides an introduction to the question of how new technology came to be a significant life event for the disabled worker. Chapters 8 and 9 represent the nucleus of the qualitative analysis of disabled workers' experiences of new technology. These chapters aim to explore qualitatively the benefits of new technology, the nature of workplace barriers, and the relationship between the two. Chapter 8 appraises the benefits new technology has provided for disabled people. Chapter 9 tempers much of the optimism engendered by the previous chapter by revealing the continued barriers to an enabling use of new technology. It also reveals how new technology is only as beneficial as the surrounding configuration of barriers allows.

An overview of Part 3

Part 3 draws together the theoretical and empirical facets of this work. In Chapter 10 conclusions are provided which draw out the essential ideas to come out of the study. The conclusions also include an appraisal of the validity of a barriers approach as a new paradigm for disability research. In Chapter 11, the final chapter, policy points will be made with the aim of using the research findings to inform new policy initiatives in the field of new technology and the employment of disabled people. Such a policy approach is explicit about going beyond simply theorizing the relationship between new technology, employment and disability: it actively attempts to ensure that thesis become praxis.

PART 1

ISSUES IN ENABLING TECHNOLOGY

 1

Disability and new technology: a barriers approach

This book explores critically the role new technology may be playing in enabling disabled people to use their abilities more fully in the field of employment. This question will be viewed in two ways. Firstly, what immediate role can new technology play in opening up the employment environment, and what factors are likely to limit this process? Secondly, in what ways might new technology allow a redefinition of disability itself? That is, in what ways does new technology produce altered perceptions of the source of disablement, given its potential to redefine workplace barriers? The thrust of this work is that while new technology can be seen to offer the potential of more enabling employment environments (Giannini 1981; Sandhu 1987), the way that new technology is experienced cannot be understood in a social and theoretical vacuum, and that these experiences will themselves be heavily influenced by the historical barriers that have shaped disabled people's wider educational, training and employment experiences (Finkelstein 1980; Barton and Tomlinson 1981; Barnes 1990a; Oliver 1990). That is, the design, use and level of access to technology will all be influenced by some aspect of this configuration of barriers.

There are two important reasons for framing the research in this way. Firstly, the predominant model of thinking about new technology and disabled people has previously come from ideas grounded in a rehabilitation model of disability and new technology (Hazan 1981; Schofield 1981; Stevenson and Sutton 1983; Cornes 1984, 1987, 1989, 1990; Ashok et al. 1985; Floyd and North 1985; Rajan 1985a; Moses 1988; Carew and West 1989; Gibler in Perlman and Hansen 1989; Busby 1990; MacFarlane 1990; Murray and Kenny 1990). It will be argued that within this rehabilitation or deficit model, new technology and its impact on the working lives of disabled people is viewed unproblematically. By simply providing new technology, this model assumes, disabled workers will be unambiguously assisted. Here new technology and its beneficial function is considered in a social vacuum. In this model, the solution to disability is technical, not social. In this sense, much previous research can be characterized in terms of what the American sociologist C. Wright-Mills termed 'abstracted empiricism', namely, research which ignores the social context of its research subjects and which denies or ignores its theoretical underpinnings (C. Wright-Mills 1959: 60–86). Even a cursory analysis of the deficit model of disability and technology suggests it is premised on a form of technological determinism; that is, new technology and its increased presence in the working environment will be an inherently beneficial development for disabled people. (On technological determinism see Elliot and Elliot 1976; MacKenzie and Wajcman 1985; Finnegan *et al.* 1987; Gill 1985; Lyon 1988.) The other key reason for re-evaluating research in this area is that within a deficit model, new technology becomes beneficial at the point at which it begins to correct the deficits of the disabled person. The site of significance and the disability problem is clearly identified as the individual and their impairment.

In contrast to a deficit model, this book explicitly adopts a social barriers model of disability. By focusing on the broader configuration of factors that surround the experience of new technology, and in seeing the main benefit of technology in its impact on these barriers, this model draws the emphasis away from the individual to the configured barriers disabled people face. The essential thrust of this work, then, is that only by adopting a social barriers approach to studying the experiences of disabled people using new technology in employment can we really understand the processes concerned. In policy terms, only by adopting a social barriers approach can enabling policies be formulated around new technology and disabled workers.

The centrepiece of this book is a national study of disabled workers using new technology, one which draws on a social barriers model of disability and which counters all previous deficit model research in this field. The research findings vindicate the strength of a social barriers model both in understanding and providing rich insights into the lives of disabled people. Reframing research into a social barriers framework educes very different findings and provides more-enabling insights; it challenges, and, hopefully overturns the long-established hegemony of the medical model of disability and its subsidiaries. In order to understand more fully the remit and theoretical approach of this book, discussion begins with a definition of the key terms used and then explores further the very different implications of deficit and social barriers models when applied to the question of disability, employment and new technology.

Defining terms

Disability

An important task at this stage is to define the terminology used and to orient the reader to the remit of the study. For the purpose of this book disability is

taken to mean the socially produced barriers that are the result of wider attitudes and structures that limit a person with a physical impairment (UPIAS
1976; Barnes 1990a; Oliver 1990: 11. Compare with Wood 1981). In this way it
views disablement as a socially constructed oppression, and not as a personal
problem. A social barriers approach (as the name suggests) identifies barriers
in wider society, and the way in which these same barriers limit the everyday
lives of people with impairments. This approach is not a departure from the
established social model of disablement; it does, however, strongly emphasize
the need to address the specific barriers that continue to disable people with
impairments.

Impairment

An impairment is here defined as any limitation or difference resulting from
a physical and/or sensory condition. Impairment is not taken to be synonymous with disability but is simply a precursor to the wider disabling
processes that follow from such a physical deviation from the norm.
Although impairment is not theoretically implicated in the disabling process,
the experience and perception of impairment is seen to be of significance for
this work. This is an unorthodox, but not entirely novel approach (see Morris
1991: 10; French in Swain *et al.* 1993: 17–26), one which is grounded in the
notion that the social model, in attempting to separate the personal (impairment) from the social (disablement), may be underplaying important
nuances in the relationship between impairment and disability.

   This is far from arguing that disability is the result of individual impairment; it does claim, however, that a careful reclaiming of the personal is
important given the significance of impairment/physical difference in the
everyday lives of disabled people. This approach need not weaken the broader
impact of a barriers model, indeed it will help make connections between
experiences at the personal and structural levels and draw upon past research
exploring the personal experiences of disability and impairment (Ashley
1974; Weiner 1975; Davidson in Brechin *et al.* 1981; Thomas 1982; Locker
1983; French 1988; Oliver *et al.* 1988; Morris 1989; Lonsdale 1990; Taylor and
Bishop 1991). The confidence invested in a social barriers model of disability
can be seen to provide insights from the experience of impairment that will
inform disability studies. The issue here is one of primacy: here social barriers
are unequivocally identified as the primary factor in disablement. Indeed,
where the term 'disabled' is used it is expressing a political power relation. It is
synonymous with the term 'oppressed' (Abberley 1987) and cannot be viewed
as purely adjectival, but as a fully relational concept, one where the word 'disabled' has to be placed in relation to disabling factors (see Finkelstein 1980:
16–28). A social barriers model, if it is to improve our understanding of disabled people's lives, also has to acknowledge that a number of disabled people
will have absorbed able-bodied ideologies which emphasize disability as a
personal tragedy.

Employment

Employment in the research for the book has been confined to white-collar settings. This was a conscious decision based on two key factors. Firstly, such settings offer the greatest potential for disabled people in terms of environmental control and technological diffusion. In this sense, white-collar work was viewed as the acid test for the assessment of the enabling potential of new technology. Secondly, it was an attempt to exclude those employment settings that approximated to established blue-collar working regimes (Littler 1984; Salaman in Deem and Salaman 1985: 1–21) such as warehouse and factory work, which have been in rapid decline during the past 30 years (Hamnett *et al.* 1989: 245). There are, however, anomalous employments that defy easy categorization, but which are included for the purposes of this study. One example is laboratory work. Here discretion was exercised, and inclusion was based on whether or not the person's work was predominantly text-based. That is, laboratory workers using new technology whose work was mainly, by their own definition, paper- or text-based, came within the remit of the study. Employment more generally was taken to mean any paid work, full- or part-time, and includes disabled people who are self-employed (people working on an own-account basis but not themselves employers). In all instances these self-employed participants had been employees. Also, because the study attempted to explore experiences over time, unemployed ex-employees were also included. To exclude unemployed participants would have been to deny a voice to an already silent constituency of disabled people (Oliver in Brown and Scase 1991: 132). This approach also enhances the range of experiences of new technology included in this research.

One important distinction made for analytical purposes was that made between *computer workers* and *technology users*. Here, computer workers were identified as those who work as computer programmers, analysts and engineers: that is, their work would not exist were it not for the advent of new technology; their work is predominantly focused around new technology itself. Technology users, in contrast, are workers doing a variety of jobs such as clerical, administrative, research, laboratory, supervisory and managerial work. In this area new technology has superseded formerly manual or mechanical working methods and is now widely used as an adjunct to most contemporary work practice.

New technology

For the purposes of this book, the term 'new technology' is a broad inclusive category which includes technology based on integrated circuitry; it covers mainstream, off-the-peg technology and specialized technologies purposely designed to allow disabled workers to function in a conventional work setting. These forms of new technology are commonly referred to as third-wave technologies (Toffler 1980; Lyon 1988) and include both information and communications technologies. The term 'new technology' is preferred to the more nebulous 'computer technology' and the more value-laden 'high technology'.

The rehabilitation or deficit model

Because rehabilitation writers and practitioners have been at the forefront in the field of technology assessment, and have been largely responsible for the optimism placed in new technology, it is important to address the approach in outline to provide a sense of how academic discussion has been dominated by and rooted in medical and para-medical world views. The basic premise of the rehabilitation model of new technology is that it succeeds in either attenuating the physical or sensory problems the disabled person has (note that the word 'disabled' is used to mean actual impairment within the rehabilitation approach), or that it augments the person, who because of a disability has not attained the normal and accepted range of abilities.

Thus the deficit model is clearly a subsidiary form of the medical model of disability. This understanding of the role of new technology can usefully be termed a *deficit* model, as its premises are based upon the notion that technology would not be significant except for its impact on the deficits of the disabled person. Technology, then, has a corrective function, one that corrects an individual's personal shortcomings.

The deficit model and the labour market

The deficit model can be better understood if placed within a wider context, that of labour market analysis. Using the tenets of this approach, and recognizing that the key proponents of the model are rehabilitation workers, the main function of new technology is that of enhancing a supply of employment-ready disabled people. This is the key role of technology (Stevenson and Sutton 1983). Here the affinity between the individualizing of the deficit model and the supply-side emphasis of labour market theory can be seen to dovetail theoretically. Within a deficit model the failure of employers to employ (unemployment), to employ adequately (underemployment) and to retain employees, is caused by the inadequate process of correction of the deficits of disabled people. This approach has also been used to explain the unemployment problems that have beset some able-bodied workers; this, however, is couched in general terms as a skills crisis (for a discussion see Marsh and Vogler in Gallie *et al.* 1994). Where disabled people are concerned, the reliance upon an individual deficit model suggests a clear course of action to try to continue the correction of deficits. New technology is clearly seen as important in this process.

A principal theoretical objective of this book is to counter a deficit model of new technology and disabled people by adopting a *social barriers* model. The notion of a social barriers model of disablement is not new (Bowe 1978;

Finkelstein in Oliver 1991: 30; Swain *et al.* 1993). The application of this approach to new technology and employment, however, is a new development in disability studies.

A social barriers model (in contrast to a deficit model) can be seen to fit with a demand-side emphasis on the deficits of the employment environment. Here, the inadequate employment demand for disabled people is due to the disabling nature of the employment environment and to negative employer attitudes to people with impairments. The key postulate of such a model is that a wholesale rehabilitation of the workplace needs to occur if the potential of formerly excluded disabled people is to be realized. While new technology may be able to play a significant part in this rehabilitation, it alone cannot be expected to furnish the changes required to create a fully enabling employment environment. It is unlikely that such a wholesale improvement in employment environments could begin to develop more generally under the canopy of a disabling society.

Applying a social barriers model

Despite the severe inadequacies of the deficit model, it would be wrong to suggest that its optimism about new technology is inappropriate or overstated. The identification, however, of the benefits of new technology as constructed and expressed by disabled people themselves is of crucial importance. By ignoring the breadth of experiences of technology, and by assuming disabling premises in theorizing the role of technology, no real advance in our understanding is possible. The value of new technology within a social barriers approach is its potential to redefine the three major barriers facing disabled people in the workplace, namely environmental, attitude and technical barriers.

Environmental barriers

By amalgamating a variety of tasks into a small workstation, new technology can create a microcosmic working environment. That is, it can bring a number of diverse tasks such as inputting data, collating data (filing), manipulating data, transmitting data, retrieving data, communicating with separate databases, and monitoring the performance of the user. Here not only is there potential for reducing the physical demands of the workplace – the need to traverse long distances, to handle heavy files, to process a large number of paper transactions – there is also the potential to bring an increasing number of functions and skills into one coordinated and focused work location. This process can be seen as allowing employment to be more readily accessible to disabled workers.

Environmental barriers and communication

To this point the potential benefits of new technology have been framed within a concern for enhanced physical control of the employment environment. A related concern is the extent to which new technology may enhance communication. The development of electronic mail and of facsimile devices allows for the rapid communication of data and messages via a non-voice format. Although most people will use these devices as an adjunct to speech, the potential exists for mainstream hardware and applications to enable workers with speech impairments to communicate facts and ideas in a form they choose. It may also allow the communication of abilities in a quite unique way.

Environmental barriers and specialized technology

Although the principle of reducing environmental barriers remains the same with both mainstream and specialized technology, the reasons for introducing the latter may be different to those for the former, with some specialized technology being provided according to a needs-based philosophy, to use Stone's distinction between needs- and work-based distributive systems (Stone 1985). Also the relationship between specialized technology and impairment may be unique, in that some users would not benefit from mainstream technologies.

Examples of the potential benefits of specialized technologies are devices which allow non-conventional forms of input, manipulation and output of data; although a thorough assessment of equipment is not appropriate here (see Schofield 1981; Church and Glennen 1992), the basic principles of these devices may help clarify their particular significance. Input devices include alternatives to the depression of conventional keys on a keyboard using: puff or blow devices, electronic wands, keyboard matrix (which are large grid-like displays allowing the selection of PC functions by sequential pressing), joystick operation and scalloped keyboards which provide access for people with impaired hands. Developments have also taken place in the field of voice activation, allowing data input by people with dexterity impairments and people with visual impairments. Braille keyboards, optical document scanners and speech output devices also benefit users with visual impairments; speech output devices allow both feedback on work in progress and a speech copy of what is about to be printed. Braille printers also provide an alternative to the conventional type of printer.

Attitude barriers

While the above represent possible routes into a previously exclusive employment environment, technology can also be seen perhaps more fundamentally as a challenge to the attitudes held about people with impairments.

How is this possible? Broadly, technology has the potential to allow formerly excluded and discounted abilities to surface. By providing a greater plurality of means of expression, the scope for the realization of abilities could in turn produce an altered perception of disabled people. Because attitudes are the principal source of many other barriers, the significance of attitude change cannot be overstated.

Technical barriers

Technical barriers refer to work-based equipment and processes that have previously excluded or hampered disabled people in the employment arena. Manual keyboards, Gestetner copiers and microfiche viewers are all examples of technical equipment that has excluded workers with physical and visual impairments. New technology's size, electronic switching and portability allow the potential for more user-friendly operation. A particular benefit stems from the development of electronic keyboards that make typing more manageable than earlier manual and electric forms. The soft-touch keyboard allows people with dexterity impairments formerly limited by heavy or unwieldy keyboards to access the key communication hub of office work. The keyboard has for many years provided an alternative to the production of text using a pen; only now with the development of easy-to-use keyboards can this progression be fully appreciated, even by those with no formal keyboard skills. This particular form of keyboard represents a major if unplanned breakthrough in providing a plurality of data production methods for disabled workers.

It seems curious that while discussing the potential benefits of new technology, some developments may create barriers. The scope for a disabling use of new technology needs to be addressed. This double-edged character of new technology is one example of its problematic nature. The pace of technical change has meant that the impact on workers has been chaotic and wide-ranging. Nowhere more than the field of technology and technical change has the notion of planned obsolescence and market-driven change been more obvious. The result of this has been the development of hardware and software, which although setting trends which may fit with the aims of disabled people, is in turn, subject to further technological change and possibly obsolescence (Freeman 1974). A recent example is that of the increased use of graphics, both as a selling point for the technology, and as the latest word in office practice. Unfortunately, the implications for people with visual impairments are that many are systematically excluded from using graphics as programs to date do not allow the translation of graphics into Braille or speech output form. Perhaps it is a retrograde step for some disabled workers that graphics packages are increasingly being produced and adopted without thought to users who rely upon the three-dimensional manipulation of their screen content.

Conclusion

This chapter has suggested that there is a growing body of literature discussing the potential benefits of new technology for disabled people in the employment arena. However, such discussion has to date been monopolized by what can usefully be termed a deficit model, one promulgated by rehabilitation professionals. There is a clear challenge to this approach – a social barriers model. This new model is seen as more likely to provide an enabling framework with which to understand the possible benefits of new technology for disabled workers and job seekers. However, a key part of this application of a social barriers model is a recognition that new technology not only allows potential benefits for disabled people, but that technological change is itself influenced by the wider matrix of social barriers. In Chapter 2 we will begin to look at the discourse that has grown up around the promise of new technology. We shall aim to identify how such perspectives are heavily (if implicitly) rooted in wider political philosophies.

 **2**

The promise of new technology

This chapter discusses the broader social, economic, occupational and technological changes underlying the specific potential of new technology for disabled workers. We can usefully distinguish three distinct theoretical frameworks for understanding this promise.

Firstly, technicism concentrates on the momentous changes in the nature of technology itself, rather than the economic and social changes that are coterminous with such technical change. Secondly, we can identify what might be dubbed a right-wing political perspective on the promise of technology. This approach is favoured by a number of rehabilitation writers, and relies heavily on theories of post-industrialism and technological determinism. Thirdly, left-wing or radical perspectives rely on a wider discussion of links between technical, economic and social change, acknowledging the importance of all of these factors in realizing the potential of new technologies for disabled workers. In reality, perspectives may draw on more than one of these typifications.

Despite their differences, most commentaries on the promise of new technology (Bowe 1980; Finkelstein 1980; Hawkridge and Vincent 1985; Cornes 1987: 2–5, 1989: 2–3; Leclerque and Deghaye 1988; Moses 1988: 7; Chamot in Perlman and Hansen 1989: 10–14; MacFarlane in British Computer Society 1990: 87) take a historical and often quasi-evolutionary view of technological change. This ordinarily involves a comparison of the nature of employment before, during and after the industrial revolution. We begin, however, by looking at what has been called a technicist approach to the promise of technology.

We can begin to understand this discourse by addressing the influential work of David Hawkridge and Tom Vincent. They provide a characteristic technicist appraisal of how technological change can be mapped and understood (Hawkridge and Vincent 1985: 43; see also Giannini 1981; Hazan 1981). They draw on Stonier's work in suggesting that old or mechanical technology extended musculature, while new technology extends the nervous system (Stonier 1983). While this biological analogy is clearly simplistic, given that the latter also extends the musculature, it serves to highlight the essential difference between mechanical and microchip technologies.

Although broadly apolitical, the work of Hawkridge and Vincent makes an important point, one featuring more widely in the literature: microchip technology, like the Copernican revolution, calls in question ergonomic assumptions about the human body, technology and the wider environment. Although not designed to enhance the quality of working life per se, the size and interactive nature of new technology is a clear contrast with the dehumanized image of the factory and mechanical technologies. This simple but essential point has to feature in any analysis of the potential of new technology.

In contrast to Hawkridge and Vincent, the seminal work of Vic Finkelstein explicitly connects the potential of new technology with a left political analysis of social and industrial change (Finkelstein 1980: 8–21). For Finkelstein the possibility of enabling technology is substantially aided by the ebbing of the capitalist factory system. However, it is important to note that industrial change is the necessary but insufficient prerequisite for enabling technology. Parallel changes in social attitudes to disability are cited as central to an enabling society (Finkelstein 1980). Implicit in Finkelstein's work is the need for enabling professional practice (see Drake in Barton 1996: 162–3), and a vibrant disability movement (Driedger 1989; Shakespeare 1993) as necessary concomitants of these wider changes. How then does Finkelstein construct a left version of technological promise?

Prior to capitalist industrialization, in what Finkelstein dubbed phase one of his historical analysis of social and technical change, disabled people often contributed to the economy, and although culturally marginalized were seen as an integral part of many agricultural and small craft-production processes. The industrial revolution and the demands of industrial capitalism, what Finkelstein referred to as phase two of his historical schema, translated into a mass form of production. Here production was geared to economies of scale, was dislocated from the worker's home and community; the harsh demands of a factory system relied increasingly on the notion of an average worker. 'Average' equated to an ability to output a quantity of work equal to the fittest worker. (For a detailed and less schematic assessment see Marx 1954: 590–2; Thompson 1967: 56–97; Landes 1969; Kumar 1978: 64–149; Littler 1982.) In this way, factory machinery and processes assumed the average worker into its very rhythm and design.

The wholesale exclusion of disabled people from the industrial scene inevitably had the wider effect of constructing disabled people as a population apart, as an unproductive problem population (Finkelstein 1980: 10; Sokolowska in Albrecht 1981; Stone 1985; Gleeson 1991). The social fallout from this process was the development of engrained negative attitudes towards disabled people (Finkelstein 1980; Gleeson 1991) and physical barriers in work and the wider social environment.

The historical ebbing of the factory system, the major changes in technology described by Hawkridge and Vincent above (see also Francis 1986; Forester 1989), and the growth of white-collar work characteristic of a post-industrial society (Hamnett *et al.* 1989) led Finkelstein to assert that new technology, if accompanied by the requisite attitude and social change, has the potential to allow a fundamental redefinition of the nature of work. This Finkelstein called phase three of his historical schema.

The advent of new technologies allows for a reversal of many of the processes that accompanied capitalist industrialization. The size, portability and range of functions embodied in personal computers suggest that previously large physical workplace and heavy work practices can now be performed in what might be termed the microcosmic environment of new technology. Relatedly, the merging of computing with communication systems allows the clear possibility of homeworking.

The momentous changes noted above provide scope for a redefinition of paid work. Clearly the notion of an average worker is not embodied in new workplace technologies in the way that it was in industrial machinery (although it may be in certain work processes, for example typing speeds). The apparently inexorable shift from home to dislocated factory can now be viewed as simply a chapter in our social and economic history. Additionally, the very different modus operandi of much new technology work holds the potential for a redefinition and awareness of the skills and abilities of disabled workers. For Finkelstein, however, the potential benefits of new technologies are clearly contingent on the wider social changes needed to counter the exploitative and divisive nature of a capitalist society.

We could assert that although society is becoming post-industrial through time, Finkelstein does not equate a post-industrial society with the assumptions of post-industrial theorists. For him post-industrial society is simply a society in which industrial work is no longer dominant and microtechnological developments bring about very different forms of (white-collar) work; *post-industrialism*, however, embraces both a description of these changes and an optimistic political philosophy which views this post-industrial shift as inherently progressive (see below).

Finkelstein's early commentary is not without its problems. Finkelstein's discussion of technological change clearly echoes Marx's quasi-evolutionary schema of socio-economic and technological change; however, it is not entirely clear from his analysis to what extent capitalism has to change for enabling technology to be maximized (see Oliver 1990:124–5). It is also not clear whether technological change is seen as an autonomous development from capitalism, nor whether technology is the main factor in producing qualitative changes in the nature of work in a capitalist society. In this way it is very difficult to plot the enabling potential of technological change while no predictive formula for the changes required within capitalism are forthcoming. As Finkelstein's more recent work seems to imply, technological, work and environmental change might take place beneath the existing canopy of capitalist economic relations (Finkelstein and Stuart in Hales 1996:170–87).

Additionally, critics have questioned the accuracy of some of Finkelstein's historical assertions encapsulated in his three phases (Meyerson and Scruggs in Finkelstein 1980: 59–67). Here Meyerson and Scruggs point to Finkelstein's simplistic treatment of these phases. They pose the question: can we really assume that the deleterious shift from phase one to two was the same for all disabled people or were those disabled people with historically the most meagre social resources, the most disadvantaged by the shift to industrial production? Meyerson and Scruggs also ask: is the utopian image of phase three a balanced prognosis or wishful thinking? While these are cogent points, this book accepts the basic value of Finkelstein's essentially heuristic phases, while trying to build on his work by addressing the interplay of technological change and social barriers.

Rehabilitation writers adopt a similar optimistic appraisal of the historical role of new technology (Stevenson and Sutton 1983; Cornes 1987, 1989; Sandhu 1987). This approach can be termed a right or liberal appraisal of the benefits of new technology. Although often implicit, the optimism inhering in this professionally-driven approach stems from a belief that not only is the nature of work changing, but also the nature of capitalism. Taking their cue from the post-industrial theory of Daniel Bell (1974, 1980) and Clark Kerr (1962), they base their notions of promise on a belief in the total revolutionizing of production: both the method of production, and what is being produced. Of significance for disabled people is the notion contained within post-industrialism, that the main focus or dynamic of post-industrial society is information. In this way an information society has profound implications for those previously excluded from a production process based upon physical prowess, muscular normality and manipulation of objects.

Post-industrial theory suggests immense promise for disabled people, in that a society based on information would not only suggest that access to the stuff of social life and work would be easier with new technology, but that information is power. Post-industrialists support their assertions by comparing the ownership and control of factory machinery with the ease of control (a term used unproblematically) of new technology and information. Within this model, new technology, its diffusion and influence, is a concomitant of political and social change away from industrialism, modernism and the remnants of the factory system. Unlike Finkelstein, where benefits accrue from the changing relationship between disability, technology and the environment, for post-industrialists it is argued that the shift to information produces profound changes in social power relations. While this sounds even more promising for disabled people, the degree of optimism post-industrialism radiates is a warning of the possible political naiveté with which it operates.

Profound shortcomings can be identified within a post-industrialist model of society and social change, not least its implicit assumption that society would become post-capitalist (see Kumar 1978; Kivisto 1981; Cohen and Zysman in Forester 1989; Gorz 1990: 66–90). A related problem within post-industrial theory is its reliance on a form of technological determinism, which is a theory of social change which assumes that technical change drives social change – a highly questionable assertion. This model, however, has influenced the thinking of many commentators.

The promise of new technology explored

In discussing the promise of new technology for disabled people, commentators emphasize variously the rapid spread of new technology, and its eventual ubiquity, as likely to open up more opportunities for disabled people. A recent report on civil servants with visual impairments by the government's Central Communications Technology Agency (1989: 4) stated: 'Indeed, as more and more organisations use computers as essential tools of carrying out their work, it should open up a wider range of jobs for people with a visual handicap' (Carew and West 1989).

In a similar, but more general observation, Giannini notes: 'The handicapped individual today can engage in fields such as data processing, accounting and bookkeeping; fields of gainful employment in which there is considerable outside contact' (in Hazan 1981: 12).

More specific comments relate to the low cost of technology (Hazan 1981: 9), to enhanced self-esteem (Sandhu 1987: 600) and to the role technology might have in allowing greater autonomy in a disabled person's work (Weinberg 1990: 128). One area of particular interest to writers in this field is the potential new technology allows for homeworking. The scope for home-based work, alluded to in the earlier discussion of post-industrialism, is seen to be an exciting development. In allowing work based at home, scope exists for saving valuable energy in getting to, from and around the place of work. The development of communications technology allows remote working and the transmission of work to a central point, for example via modems, e-mail and fax. This would allow for home-based work without compromising the level of contact with the employing organization. Here the convergence of microchip technology with telecommunications (information technology or telematics) promises both new ways of working and a dramatic rise in information work (but see Gill 1985: 37–62, and Lyon 1988 for a critical appraisal of this latter assertion). The development of fibre optic video communications is an obvious example of this potential.

Homeworking, teleworking, telecommuting are all variations on this theme, a theme especially important for workers with severe mobility and sensory impairments. As Murray and Kenny note in their study of the experiences of disabled teleworkers, 'telework will create new opportunities for people with severe disabilities [*sic*], as well as enabling others who become disabled during employment to retain their jobs' (Murray and Kenny 1990: 206). The literature of promise is replete with this level of optimism, and prognostications are offered with a degree of incaution uncharacteristic of academic commentary. Hawkridge again provides a good example of this in stating:

There is little doubt that by AD 2000 many more disabled adults will be able to work at home if they wish. Computer-based terminals will be so ubiquitous that a blind adult say, will have little difficulty in carrying out a wide variety of activities in the home. A deaf person will converse quite freely about work by telephone, possibly with speech impaired friends.

(Hawkridge and Vincent 1985: 238)

The former Minister for Disabled People, Nicholas Scott, shared this sense of unbridled optimism when he noted that unlimited prospects for the future exist for disabled people using new technology (cited by Cornes in Oliver 1991: 98). In support of the above optimistic assessments of the potential role of technology are studies suggesting the large-scale diffusion of technology. Not only is new technology now more widely spread than say ten years ago, it seems almost inevitable that this spread of new technology and new applications will continue into the third millennium. Kling and Iacono's study of desktop computerization in the United States is indicative of the increased diffusion of new technology. Their findings suggested that by 1985, 20 per cent of the American white-collar workforce were using terminals or microcomputers, and that the yearly rate of growth of PC use will be 15 per cent (Kling and Iacono in Forester 1989: 336–7).

New technology is by the 1990s much more an integral part of the collective consciousness of white-collar workers. Indicative of this rapid change was a *Times* poll conducted in 1982, in which only 20 per cent of the respondents claimed to know what information technology was (in Hawkridge and Vincent 1985: 41). One would predict a significantly higher figure in the 1990s. This widespread perception of the growth of new information technologies is provided in Kenneth Baker's Panglossian statement of 1982:

The age of information technology . . . has arrived. I know of no other technological advantage which has brought together so many areas of rapid and exciting development. Computers and telecommunications are converging rapidly . . . the impact of information technology will be felt at every level in our society.

(in Lyon 1988: 22)

An empirically reliable measure of the diffusion of new technology is provided by Daniel (1987). This study of 2000 British organizations found that 61 per cent of employees and managers reported a major expansion of their computing base, a similar figure was recorded for word processor use.

As well as the technological change noted above are the structural shifts away from blue-collar toward white-collar work, away from manufacturing toward service occupations (Gallie 1988: 4) and the concomitant increase of women workers in the British labour force (Hakim 1979, 1987).

Based on the above evidence it would be tempting to adopt a straightforwardly optimistic appraisal of new technology and its potential for disabled people. A major limitation of such optimistic evaluations are that in relying on post-industrial visions of both left- and right-wing varieties, the complexities that surround the relationship between technology, employment and disabled people may be overlooked. One important example of this is the failure to separate mainstream from specialized technologies in the discussion of the promise of new technology.

Much analysis of the promise of new technology relies on two key assumptions: firstly, that the large-scale diffusion of new technology will extend to specialized technology in the same way as mainstream technologies. Secondly, it is assumed that in the British context the state, not the market, will predominate in this provision. Both of these assertions can be challenged. There is no legitimate reason to assume that the diffusion of specialized technologies will follow the pattern of the spread of off-the-peg technologies. Each operates by very different dynamics. It is also erroneous to assume that the state is *the* arbiter of specialized new technology. Although commonly accessed through a needs-based system (Stone 1985), the design, accessibility and cost of specialized technology is the result of competitive market forces, and its makers and suppliers are likely to work squarely within the deficit model of disability. This has implications for any appraisal of specialized technology that assumes it to be inherently beneficial, or free from the constraints of a market economy. Although a detailed and critical exploration of the theoretical issues at stake in the above conflation of mainstream and specialized technology is beyond the scope of this work, attention will be drawn in the empirical findings of this research to the relationship between state and market in the provision of specialized technologies.

Conclusion

There are myriad accounts of the potential of new technology to enhance the employment experiences of disabled people. However, evidence suggests that an interest in such developments in no way guarantees that these potential benefits will materialize. Technicists' evaluations of the changing character of technology provides perhaps the least contested ideas around the promise of new technology; but this perspective fails to connect technical with socio-political change (Hawkridge and Vincent 1985). The left post-industrial schema of Finkelstein (1980) and the right post-industrialism of much rehabilitation writing (Giannini 1981; Hazan 1981; Stevenson and Sutton 1983; Cornes 1987, 1989; Sandhu 1987; Chamot in Perlman and Hansen 1989; MacFarlane 1990) both fail to grasp completely the interplay of social, economic and technological forces.

Only by understanding these interrelated factors can we begin to predict with some accuracy the extent to which technological promise is likely to materialize into technological reality. However, it is the radical ideas of Finkelstein which inform this work most directly. Finkelstein's work clearly demands that the wider influence of attitudes, barriers and the action of disabled people are all essential factors in shaping the enabling role of new technology.

While the above analysis has been concerned with the broad changes likely to facilitate the realization of technology benefits, the next chapter explores the specific benefits of new technology in the lives of individual disabled people. The chapter illustrates the research to date in this area, and points to the dominance of rehabilitation writers in defining the problem of disability and the solution of new technology.

 **3**

Researching new technology: the road to nowhere?

This chapter examines research already undertaken in the field of new tech-nology and the employment of disabled people. The essential message of this chapter is that research to date has failed to provide an adequate theory of the role new technology plays in the lives of disabled workers. This, it is argued, has in turn led to shallow and one-dimensional research methodolo-gies. It will be argued that the research methods and the focus of research are directly linked to the rehabilitation or deficit model of the disability problem. Clearly, the theoretical framework adopted will shape the nature of the research itself; as John Hughes notes in his *The Philosophy of Social Research*: 'every research tool or procedure is inextricably embedded in commitments to particular versions of the world and knowing the world' (Hughes 1990: 11).

By applying a deficit model to researching disability, the design, process and findings of these studies has obscured the relationship between disability, the body and the environment, and in some instances can be seen to have applied disabling assumptions and practices. It is possible to analyse the spread of seemingly diverse studies on new technology and disability to extract common theoretical and methodological approaches.

Theoretical premises

The majority of research in the area of new technology and disabled people has been of a supply-side orientation, that is, it asks: what effect has new technology had on the employability of disabled people? Here, the emphasis is on the way new technology might reduce the 'deficits' the disabled person may have, and thus enhance employment opportunities by improving dis-abled people's marketability. The assumption is that the problem being cor-rected is the disabled individual and that the benefits of new technology are simply an extension of the wider benefits of the rehabilitation role: that of 'improving' the impaired individual. The following quote, taken from the research of the influential deficit model writer Paul Cornes, captures the general spirit of the deficit model favoured by rehabilitation writers. Once the general principle of the model is understood, it is possible to see how new technology is just one tool in what might be dubbed the 'repertoire of improvement':

> The case studies suggest that highly motivated, properly trained and equipped young people can and do overcome such [employment] obstacles and that their success in doing so may encourage employers to adopt more favourable attitudes toward people with similar disabilities.
>
> (Cornes 1989: 34)

Cornes establishes clearly the *raison d'être* of rehabilitation workers, that of facilitating the supply of well-trained and motivated disabled people. It is worth noting the tone of this quote, one which contains an air of exhortation which clearly establishes the disabled person as the problem in the unemployment equation. It is possible to contrast this with a demand-side model of disabled people's unemployment, one which states that insufficient employer demand is at least in part the reason for disabled people's low rates of employment. Such demand-side assumptions are rare in deficit model research, however, and perhaps surprisingly such sentiments do appear in Cornes's own work, for example when he states:'Nevertheless there is a clear indication in the data gathered from this study that employers remain resistant to the employment of people with disabilities [*sic*], about whom many stereotyped perceptions and inappropriate expectations persist' (Cornes 1989: 33).

Here, Cornes shifts from identifying disabled people as the required locus of change to a rather contradictory stance of suggesting that employers remain a barrier to disabled people's employment. Arguably this contradiction stems from his position in rehabilitation studies. We can observe how although Cornes begins to adopt a critical perspective on employers, he is constantly drawn back to the deficits of disabled people (Cornes 1984, 1987, 1989, 1990; Floyd and North 1985: 12; MacFarlane 1990: 178–80). Clearly, if rehabilitation workers attenuated their deficit assumptions and began to focus much more on the inadequate demand for disabled workers, they would go beyond their narrow professional role of measuring deficits to a wider political role. Recent evidence from critical writers in rehabilitation studies acknowledges the political risk of adopting a more demand-side emphasis on recalcitrant employers (Stubbins 1987; Vandergoot 1987). Rehabilitation writers are constantly reminded that their work is a branch of medicine, or a satellite of the Employment Service, and that to ask difficult questions as to why employers fail to employ disabled people would be to risk losing their own professional base.

One possible route out of the above professional dilemma is an emphasis on the changing nature of work itself; this helps explain why so many rehabilitation writers have taken an interest in the decline of industrial society and the growth of new technology use (Stevenson and Sutton 1983; Ashok *et al.* 1985; Floyd and North 1985; Rajan 1985a; Cornes 1987, 1989; Sandhu 1987; Niwa 1988; Murray and Kenny 1990). In this way rehabilitation writers can discuss optimistically the potential of new technology, without focusing on the need for employers to change. However, despite this attempt to refocus employers' attention on employment opportunities for disabled people, such writers cannot escape the power relations that exist between professionals, employers and the state. The hidden function of rehabilitation workers is that of exhorting employers to take on problem workers who they would otherwise overlook. Relatedly, medical and employment rehabilitators cannot simply cast off their dependency on disabled people for their salaries (Oliver 1990: 90–2). The political nature of the relationship between researchers and the researched in this context is a key factor limiting the aims and outcomes of deficit research.

Focusing on deficits

Having established the dominance of rehabilitation workers' voices in the field of new technology and disabled people, and having located these voices within a supply-side focus on the enhancement of individual deficits, it should now be possible to apply a deficit model to new technology itself. As noted earlier, new technology – although acknowledged by rehabilitation writers as uniquely beneficial for disabled people – is seen as simply another tool by which disabled people's deficits are corrected. Note how the relationship between new technology and wider employment environments is absent from much of the deficit model discourse. We begin our analysis of this discourse on new technology benefits with the work of Paul Cornes again, as his thoughts are perhaps the most explicit on the matter:

> The role of technology in this context therefore is to be considered from the perspective of its contributions to therapeutic procedures to restore sensory, physical or mental functioning or technical aids to augment, compensate or substitute for reduced or lost functions.
>
> (Cornes in Oliver 1991: 103)

A similar, but more specific example is provided by MacFarlane in his discussion of the potential of new technology to correct the individual's deficits:

> This is where Information Technology comes to the fore. Through its use many a brilliant mind can be released from a crippled and inhibiting carapace. Just look at Professor Stephen Hawking . . . However one does not have to be the proverbial 'egghead' . . . ordinary mortals can benefit just as much.
>
> (MacFarlane 1990: 179–91)

Cornes provides specific examples of his deficit premises when he frames the main benefits of new technology in terms of it:'Enabling persons without speech to speak', and of 'Enabling persons with paraplegia to walk' (Cornes in Oliver 1991: 103–4). Here Cornes has no reservations in extending this optimistic approach to the world of work.

However, Cornes again contradicts his essential premises when he accepts that: 'The reasons for this [increased employment in IT] appear to be much less associated with technology than with employers' attitudes, practices and procedure' (Cornes in Oliver 1991: 109).

Cornes is grappling here with the flawed nature of the deficit model. However, in framing the role of new technology as a corrective to individual deficits, Cornes never fully realizes the theoretical potential of his project. This weakness is borne out in an earlier piece of research where Cornes refers to some workers being 'too disabled' (Cornes 1989: 25) to benefit from new technology. This statement is evidence of Cornes's perception that new technology benefits inhere in its potential to alter physical bodies rather than employers and their environments. This makes Cornes's criticisms of employers ring hollow, as he himself has not understood the nature of the disability problem. By defining individuals as too disabled, Cornes is simply adopting a disabling assumption that excluded disabled people have only themselves to blame.

Another theme of the deficit model is that of 'rescue', where new technology is seen as allowing disabled people to escape their bodily problems. In this sense, overcoming may be framed as a general triumph over 'disablement'. The following quotes provide typical examples of the rescue theme:

Developments in information technology are helping more and more people overcome disabilities . . . newly available technology points the way to a time when everyone can be 'technically equal' irrespective of physical disability.

(Sandhu 1987: 600)

IT can neutralise the worst effects of many kinds of disablement
(Hawkridge cited in Rajan 1985a)

Technology is also providing the ability to manufacture devices which offset many handicaps

(Stevenson and Sutton 1983: 485)

A variation on this theme of rescue is the suggestion that new technology is unfettered by social influence and is the passport to freedom: 'IT is disability free [and is] providing independence and self reliance' (Barker 1990: 81).

The overcoming theme is sometimes applied more specifically, as is evidenced in this quotation which links overcoming with the particular benefits of home-based working: 'Telework can open up new employment opportunities for people whose disability has excluded them from the workplace' (Murray and Kenny 1990: 206).

Despite these confused premises, a veritable research industry has grown up around the question of the benefits of new technology for disabled people. It is worth reflecting on how these diverse research projects connect with the logic of a deficit model of technology benefits.

The logic of deficit research

The logic of identifying deficits, and the role of new technology in correcting these deficits, is at the heart of much rehabilitation research; perhaps the apotheosis of this approach is to be found in 'best practice' research (Cornes 1987, 1989; Murray and Kenny 1990). Best practice research embodies the central principles of a deficit model. By seeking only positive experiences of new technology and by filtering out those experiences that do not accord with 'best practice', this research method provides the clearest message for rehabilitation workers and employers alike. The message conveys the potential for new technology to rehabilitate the person with an impairment. Here the marketing of disabled people to employers involves the packaging of the best examples of technological facilitation. This can be compared to any other form of marketing which involves the presentation of ideal messages, while avoiding messages that might undermine the marketing process, hence Cornes's framing of his 1989 study as:

> a general state-of-the-art impression of the kinds of employment opportunities available for young people with severe disabilities [sic] . . . [the research] had a restricted focus on young people who were already in employment, as opposed to those who had tried and failed to do so
> (Cornes 1989: 4)

Best practice research ignores the wider social factors likely to shape employment. Another good example is the action research completed by Murray and Kenny (1990). They explored the quality of employment experiences of disabled people doing remote teleworking, with the aim of enhancing the role of teleworking in the lives of disabled people. Although Murray and Kenny identify specific negative experiences, they do not acknowledge the broader factors that have shaped homeworking more generally (Hakim 1985; Allen and Wolkowitz 1987; Pennington and Westover 1989).

In this sense the researchers can be said to have failed to ask the most significant questions in their research such as: who instigated teleworking? Why are disabled people particularly encouraged to work from remote sites? Did disabled people ask for teleworking? Here the relationship between the individual experience of remote teleworking is inadequately linked to the structural factors that have historically led to homeworking. The end result is an apolitical and ahistorical assessment of the experience of teleworking. Although some useful ideas have come out of this research, the ultimate aim of producing showcase examples and best practice images severely limits the critical potential of the research and the action that is intended to flow from it.

The above analysis has looked at those studies ostensibly offering few critical insights into the relationship between disabled workers and new technology. Discussion now shifts to research containing a more critical dimension. Unfortunately, these contributions still conform to the basic tenets of deficit model research.

The studies conducted by Ashok *et al.* (1985) for the then Greater London Council and by Rajan (1985a) for the Institute of Manpower Studies, however, explore wider employment experiences within which new technology benefits are reported. This is an advance on best practice research in that it allows negative experiences into the research. For example, both Ashok *et al.* (1985) and Rajan (1985a) highlight the role of employers' attitudes in shaping experiences of new technology. However, the theoretical significance of new technology, its relationship to barriers, and its potential for reducing barriers is not explored. It is somewhat ironic that those studies that are most in tune with the negative attitudes disabled people face, are perhaps the least transparent about their theoretical premises. It seems that to have any degree of critical content in a research project allows the broader theoretical issues to remain unexamined.

What then are the results of such critical research? In the absence of a theoretical base the research conclusions drawn by Ashok *et al.* (1985) and Rajan (1985) exhibit deficit thinking. The presence of negative attitudes, even where they limit the benefits of new technology, can simply be reappropriated by a deficit model which interprets negative attitudes as rational responses to real personal deficits. For example, like Paul Cornes, the work of Ashok *et al.* and Rajan does not explore the theoretical relationship between new technology, environments and disabled people. While emphasizing the negative attitudes and employment barriers disabled people face, new technology is still conceptualized as correcting the body, not these barriers. In this way the potential for new technology to facilitate more accessible environments and to challenge negative attitudes is overlooked.

The role of the 'expert' researcher

An important premise that can be discerned in most of the above research (here Ashok *et al.* 1985 seem to be a notable exception) is the assumption that 'expert' knowledge should have primacy over disabled people's interpretation of their own experiences. (For a critical appraisal of this and a discussion of an emancipatory research model, one which places disabled voices at the centre of research, see Oliver and also Zarb in *Disability, Handicap and Society* 1992.) Evidence of this assertion is that the voices or verbatim responses of the disabled people researched do not feature in any of the available research. This fact is remarkable given the aims of the majority of the studies to uncover some aspect of the disabled workers' experiences (Stevenson and Sutton 1983; Ashok *et al.* 1985; Rajan 1985a; Jones 1986; Cornes 1987, 1989; Murray and Kenny 1990)

While all research is bound to be edited and selected to some extent, this wholesale absence of disabled people's voices amounts to more than a simple methodological shortcoming, and can be seen as an epistemological assumption that the researcher is the person best able to choose which data to present and how to present it.

It can be argued that the absence of disabled people's voices is the result of researchers adopting professionalized assumptions about the value of expert ideas and interpretations over those of the researched. Here the researcher–researched distinction mirrors critical analysis of professional power (McKnight in Brechin *et al.* 1981; French 1988; Zarb in Oliver 1991: 177–203; Leonard 1994: 13–18) and the power relations of the research act (Oliver in *Disability, Handicap and Society* 1992). The power of 'experts', in research terms, is usually grounded in the wider professional role of the researcher, with the shift from practice to research being seen as unproblematical and in some instances natural. This assumption of expertise also rests in a view of social research as a neutral, disinterested pursuit of the truth.

Conclusion

This chapter has illustrated some of the weaknesses of adopting a deficit approach by providing brief insights into this form of research. Although methodologically diverse and occasionally critical, these studies all have a deficit model at their centre. All are limited by this approach. The next chapter will illustrate how those factors underplayed in the above research – the social barriers that inhere in contemporary society – are central to our understanding of the potential of new technology. It is only by understanding this relationship between barriers and new technology that we can begin to understand the nature of enabling technology. It is to these social barriers that we now turn.

 **4**

Unpromising environments: structured employment and technology

This chapter provides an exploration of those factors likely to continue to shape the benefits of new technology. As was stated in the Introduction, the benefits of new technology are explicable in terms of their potential to reduce the social barriers which have limited disabled people's integration into the workplace. However, these barriers may also be continuing to limit the progress of disabled people. In this sense new technology and social barriers can be seen to impact upon each other. It is this relationship that needs to be understood.

The first part of this chapter is a brief discussion of the importance of negative attitudes in shaping the structural barriers faced by disabled people in the workplace. The bulk of this chapter is an appraisal of the resulting structural barriers that characterize contemporary employment. Useful comparisons are drawn from studies of the employment barriers facing other historically less powerful social groups.

Attitudes and structures of exclusion

There is a clear consensus within disability studies that attitudes have contributed to the exclusion of disabled people from the mainstream of social and economic life (Finkelstein 1980; Barnes 1990a: 58–9; Oliver 1990: 60–77; French in Hales 1996: 151–62. For a contrast to these views see Soder 1990: 227–41). One of the main factors likely to shape the experiences of disabled people using new technology at work are the pre-existing attitudes that characterize employment milieux. Although the nature and dynamics of negative attitudes can only be fully understood in the context in which they are lived out, we can assert with some confidence that a history of economic and social exclusion from industrial society has profoundly influenced the way disabled people are viewed (Barnes 1990a: 77–80; Humphries and Gordon

1992: 117–41). However, it is worth noting that the degree to which attitudes are shaped by economic imperatives (Finkelstein 1980: 10), economic and ideological forces combined (Oliver 1990: 25–59) or cultural and historical specificities (Thomas 1982; Ingstad and Reynolds-Whyte 1995) is still an active debate, one which is beyond the remit of this book.

Although attitude barriers impact upon disabled people generally, it is important that other cross-cutting factors are acknowledged as shaping attitudes towards people with impairments. Evidence suggests that certain social groups are likely to experience specific and compound attitude and social barriers. There is for example consistent evidence that disabled women (Fine and Asch in Deegan and Brooks 1985; Lonsdale 1990: 3–10; Hanna and Rogovsky 1991: 49–63; Morris 1991: 92–101) experience difficulties not simply because of the perception of bodily difference, but as a social group who have historically been excluded from much public and paid work activity.

When addressing the difficulties women face gaining employment with new technology, it should not be forgotten that some women have only during the last 30 years obtained permanent and socially legitimate access to much higher status paid employment. The notion of multiple barriers or oppression has also been convincingly applied to other historically marginal groups, for example black disabled people (Confederation of Indian Organizations 1987; Stuart in Swain *et al.* 1993: 93–100; Vernon in Morris 1996: 48–68) and disabled lesbians and gays (Hearn in Kaufman and Lincoln 1991; Shakespeare in Barton 1996: 209–11). Other factors likely to shape the nuanced experience of negative attitudes are the nature and visibility of a person's impairment (Goffman 1968; Jowett 1982: 24–5) and the pre-existing degree of proximity between disabled and non-disabled people (Taylor and Bogdan 1989: 21–36; Gooding 1994: 90–1).

Often overlooked in any discussion of the power and dynamics of negative attitudes are the positive actions of the disability movement. This point remains to be empirically tested, but strength gained from membership of a radical disability organization is bound to have some impact on the overt and direct expression of negative attitudes to disabled people (Brisenden 1987; Goodall 1988; Driedger 1989; Shakespeare 1993). As much research remains to be completed around the question of the factors shaping the nature of attitudes towards disabled people, the most fruitful approach is to look at their impact in limiting employment for disabled people. By looking at the extensive research into employment barriers we can begin to assess the particular experiences of the disabled people working with, or trying to access, new technology.

The structuring of employment barriers

An important set of barriers can be collectively identified as structural; that is those factors in the structure of a given society that shape, in a fairly predictable way, the opportunities and limitations for a given social group. These structural barriers should not be read as separate to attitude barriers, indeed it is difficult to conceive of one without the other; however, structural barriers reflect the wider processes, practices and proscriptions that characterize a contemporary disabling society. The power and danger of these structures of exclusion are that they are by nature embedded and taken for granted. This structuring is highly significant in terms of access to employment and new technology.

A reading of available empirical research suggests that while structures of exclusion and segregation are significant in disabled people's lives (Martin *et al.* 1989: 68; Graham *et al.* 1990; Prescott-Clarke 1990; RNIB 1991), such structures do not operate in the general and immutable sense suggested for example in 'underclass' theories. (For a discussion of the merits and limits of underclass theories see Dean and also Oliver, both in Brown and Scase 1991: 23–40.) Given the range of employments disabled people occupy it seems difficult to sustain structural arguments which allow little or no scope for occupational advancement. Perhaps more convincing is a structural approach that sees some disabled people's employment as subject to particular but fluid structural barriers. However, such fluidity is easily overstated. Clues to these possible barriers can be found in available studies of occupational segregation in the experiences of women (Hakim 1979; Cockburn 1983; Dex 1985) and black workers (Wrench in Jenkins and Solomos 1987: 160–88; Lee and Loveridge 1987; Brown in Braham *et al.* 1992: 46–63; Jenkins in Braham *et al.* 1992: 148–63). Evidence also suggests that these social groups face added barriers in accessing new technology at work (Barker and Downing 1980; Science Policy Research Unit 1982; Cockburn 1983, 1985; Harvey in Lee and Loveridge 1987: 72–82). It is necessary to look at the dynamics of segregation and exclusion available in the wider social science literature on occupational structuring.

Occupational segregation

Theoretical perspectives on segregation

Some of the most insightful studies of occupational segregation have emanated from the study of the employment experiences of women (West 1982; Dex 1985) and of black workers (Brown 1984: 150–83; Jenkins in Braham *et al.* 1992: 148–63). One of the first attempts to theorize unfair employment segregation came in the form of dual labour market analysis and was exemplified by the quantitative work of Catherine Hakim (1987). Hakim's research into the gendering of employment change provided evidence of the persistence of structured divisions between core (usually male) workers and peripheral (usually female) employees. This process has continued, even with a major employment restructuring and a massive influx of female workers into the labour market (Gallie 1988: 15–17; Walby in Wood 1989:

127–9). The terms 'core' and 'periphery' illustrate for dual labour theorists the increasing division between highly rewarded, relatively secure and occupationally varied work, and marginal, relatively insecure and less rewarding work. Dual labour theories began as attempts to identify the structuring of employment into two polar categories, the core and periphery mentioned above. The theories were often linked to economistic labour market analyses, which suggested that the recruitment and retention of workers was being consciously undertaken in order to allow the peripheral workers (usually women) to be jettisoned in times of economic downturn (note the similarities with Marxist theory of a reserve army of labour). Some black workers have also been prey to this opportunistic form of labour use, and have also been more likely to face long-term exclusion from the labour market (see Ward and Cross in Brown and Scase 1991: 116–31).

Later theories place less stress on the significance of dual, dichotomous labour markets, but discuss the notion of segregated or more properly structured employment. This development has moved dual labour market theory away from pure economic assessments toward theories of how gender differences and patriarchal values shape organizational decision-making – broadly, why women get 'women's work' and men 'men's work' (Dex 1985; Walby 1986). It also addresses why women, even when achieving high status employment (lawyers, medical doctors, academics), can still face structural limitations to their advancement vis-à-vis male workers.

The discovery by Hakim (1987) that so-called horizontal segregation (where women are segregated into women-only jobs) was diminishing, but that vertical segregation (hierarchical divisions between men and women within the same occupation) was still evident, led Crompton and Sanderson to conclude that attention needed to shift to vertical (hierarchical) segregation and the reasons for its persistence (Crompton and Sanderson 1990). They felt that a mixture of poor relative qualifications, employers' recruitment and promotion policies, and (at the broadest level) structured attitudes to women workers, all served to limit the relative achievements of women workers.

This theory of labour segregation can account for the presence of disabled workers in an increasing number of employments and occupational sectors; we need, however, to be careful not to extrapolate too much from the experiences of non-disabled female workers. There are key differences in the two groups, even at a general level. For example, many women have been employed in the burgeoning service sector employment at all levels, significantly in the credentialled and expanded professions in health, education and welfare (because these fit with women's perceived servicing role – see Walby 1986).

The scope for disabled workers (female or male) entering these jobs may well be more restrictive than for non-disabled women. Firstly, as Oliver (1990: 80) suggests, aesthetic and existential anxieties are key determinants in contemporary disabling attitudes. Here frontline service sector jobs may, in emphasizing appearance, effectively exclude some disabled employees.

French's work on health professionals' attitudes to disabled colleagues might also be seen as evidence of the prejudice that can pervade health work (French 1988). Similarly, Morris's (1989) collected experiences of women with paraplegia provide evidence of health and education employers being less than helpful in returning them to jobs commensurate with their qualifications and experience. Health, education and welfare services are major employers and may prove pivotal in terms of access to technology-inclusive employment.

Another significant barrier that confronts people with impairments is the physical environment, with many buildings continuing to reflect the needs of non-disabled people (Carver and Rodda 1978; CORAD 1982; *Which?* 1989; Barnes 1991: 171–9; Hurst in Barton 1996: 137). The voluntaristic nature of the 1970 Chronically Sick and Disabled Persons Act and the limited scope of the 1985 Building regulations (M regulations), restricting environmental criteria to buildings built after 1987, suggests that many workplace environments are still likely to throw up barriers to new-technology-inclusive work. Many computing suites in educational and employment settings are located on the first floor (and above) for security reasons. This makes access to a lift a prerequisite for a wholly enabling environment. These barriers are likely to prove especially important in shaping employment opportunities with new technology. Because little research has focused on employment environments, this book aims to contribute to our understanding of how the built environment shapes disabled people's lives.

Occupational segregation and disabled people

The OPCS report *Disabled Adults: Services, Transport and Employment* (Martin *et al.* 1989) and the Social and Community Planning Research report *Employment and Handicap* (Prescott-Clarke 1990) both provide graphic illustrations of the structurally inferior employment position of disabled people. The level of employment participation of all disabled people of working age is 31 per cent. Of the remainder, approximately 35 per cent (37 per cent male and 31 per cent female) are deemed 'permanently unable to work', while about a third (33 per cent) are classified as unemployed, or as 'other' (retired early, keeping house or in education). Leaving aside the significant detail that the researchers concede that some of the 'permanently unable' group could work if suitable jobs became available, the evidence suggests that disabled people face undue levels of unemployment relative to non-disabled people. This cannot be explained by physical status alone, given the number of disabled people looking for work. Levels of unemployment vary depending on the nature of a person's impairment, age and previous occupation.

The RNIB study (1991) found that the rate of employment for people of working age with visual impairments was 30 per cent (as a percentage of all in this age group; this is 1 per cent less than disabled people generally). More disturbing still is the figure for working-age blind people: 17 per cent of the working-age blind people are employed. Even if the variables of employ-ment, training and skill are held constant for the two groups, it seems reason-able to conclude that the differentials are due to inadequate access to employment.

Disablement and socio-economic group

Not only are disabled people much more likely to be denied the chance to work, but even when employment is achieved, they are less likely to attain high status employment relative to the general population. Disabled workers have traditionally been concentrated in manual employment (Croxen 1982; Lonsdale 1986), and despite the growth of white-collar work at all levels, including professional work, disabled people are concentrated predomin-antly in the less skilled white-collar occupations. For example, only 2 per cent of all disabled workers are in the professional category (social classes A and B), as against 4 to 5 per cent in the non-disabled population. Disabled women, although reflecting women in work generally, being concentrated in white-collar work, constitute a larger proportion of the intermediate, supervisory and management jobs.

The social shaping of technology use

There is substantial evidence for the assertion that pre-existing social hier-archies shape the use of new technology and its use in the employment sphere, especially where the technology work is seen

- as an improvement over the previous means of completing work;
- where the technology is scarce or novel;
- where the technology changes work so fundamentally that it allows major organizational reviews. This usually takes the form of the established work group feeling threatened by the advent of new technologies.

This latter is borne out in the seminal work of Cynthia Cockburn in her study *Brothers*, which chronicled the technical and organizational changes that took place in Fleet Street in the 1980s. The research suggests that estab-lished work groups will use a variety of means to retain occupational control with the advent of new technology. The reason the print workers wanted con-trol in this instance was not to control new technology per se, but to ensure that cheaper women workers were not brought in with altered technology and working practices. Clearly this was the objective newspaper proprietors intended. Cockburn's work (1983) suggests that with the advent of new working practices and new technologies, the more skilled jobs that resulted from technical change were appropriated by male, formerly hot-metal workers. For Cockburn, men are usually better placed in the power structures of employment to monopolize the best jobs, and to shape the introduction of technology. They are, in short, more likely to be the technology 'winners'. A number of studies addressing the gendered nature of technological change have come to similar conclusions (Harvey in Lee and Loveridge 1987: 72).

Cockburn's work may not represent the commonalities of how new technology is first experienced, indeed the technological changes can only be viewed in terms of the broader organizational and political changes taking place in Fleet Street. However, the wider literature (Barker and Downing 1980; Science Policy Research Unit 1982; Harvey in Lee and Loveridge 1987: 72–82; Ashburner in Crompton and Sanderson 1990: 124) when read alongside Cockburn's work (1983, 1985) suggests that social hierarchies profoundly shape access to and use of new technology. The whole process of technological change has very complex repercussions which are beyond the remit of this study; it is, however, worth pointing out that more women are employed in new low paid and often low skill and part-time office jobs where new technologies have been introduced, for example computer-based telesales. This is set against a backdrop of falling male employment in formerly skilled employment (Gallie 1988: 15; Hamnett *et al.* 1989: 59). So the impact of new technology is not always ambiguously in favour of previously dominant workers; in this instance new technology displaced many of these unionized workers while creating a number of low status clerical jobs which are viewed by employers as 'women's work'.

Disabled workers, dependency and employment prospects

Up to this point the experience of new technology for disabled people has only been discussed in terms of the perceptions and behaviours of employers, managers and colleagues. Equally significant are disabled people's own self-perceptions. Low educational attainment and expectations (Booth and Swann 1987; Prescott-Clarke 1990), the experience of dependency relationships (Oliver in Barton 1989; Barnes 1990) and the compounding of dependency by unemployment (Kuh *et al.* 1988: 5) can all be seen as potential limits to employment advancement. The historical concentration of disabled people in low grade clerical, semi-skilled and unskilled work can also be seen as factors militating against the rapid and smooth assimilation of disabled people into a technology-based working environment. As Croxen (1982: 15) notes: 'A "career in disability" does not generally make for an independent autonomous thinker. Planning, communication skills, teamwork skills all require confidence and independence, which are rarely enhanced in a disabled person's life experience.'

Homeworking and new technology

A topic often linked to the post-industrial optimism around technological change is the now well-rehearsed literature exploring the potential of new technology (generally framed as information and communications technologies) for disabled people wishing to work from home (Floyd and North

1985; Department of Trade and Industry 1990; but see also Ashok *et al.* 1985 and Murray and Kenny 1990 for more cautious assessments). Structural analysis, however, would suggest that an unalloyed optimism in the potential for home-based work should be rejected. Firstly, there is no evidence that disabled people's homes are any less disabling than their workplace (Morris in Swain *et al.* 1993: 136–44). Secondly, the historical evidence on homeworking does not augur well for disabled people. The key motivants of homeworking have historically been those of production flexibility and cost reduction (Hakim 1985, 1987; Allen and Wolkowitz 1987: 91–3); what is now rather euphemistically called externalizing production costs. As Allen and Wolkowitz note in their influential study of British homeworking:

> Little is known about the work preferences of disabled people or the alternatives to homework which could be made available to them. We cannot assume that those who prescribe home working for them are right. It is an easy option, but one which leads disabled workers into grossly exploited work.
>
> (Allen and Wolkowitz 1987: 185)

Research into disabled homeworkers suggests mixed experiences, with flexible working arrangements being tempered by isolation and the costs of overheads when working from home (Huws 1984; Ashok *et al.* 1985; Murray and Kenny 1990). While none of the research attempts to deny a priori the benefits of homeworking for disabled people, the evidence does counsel caution in any study of disabled homeworkers.

Conclusion

This chapter represents a brief appraisal of those social structures likely to shape the degree to which new technology is enabling for disabled people. It has been argued that workplaces designed for and conceptualized by non-disabled people, and the attendant negative attitudes, form identifiable structures of exclusion and organizational inferiority. While not immutable, these structures have meant that disabled people have been more likely to experience a less advantaged labour market and employment position. These factors may continue to shape the extent to which disabled people gain access to work generally and new technology benefits specifically. Parallels were drawn between the employment position of women and disabled people. The experience of women provides some cautious optimism that employment marginality can be decreased. This optimism was also extended to the employment of disabled people. However, the optimism expressed was tempered by the obvious structural barriers that permeate the workplace.

One key factor likely to enhance the degree of access disabled people have to enabling employment and technology is the role and efficacy of the state in attempting to engineer more advantageous access to both work and new technology. The following chapter provides an outline discussion of the

British system of state support in the area of 'special aids to employment'. It will be argued that this scheme has done little to alter the employment disadvantage of the majority of disabled people, and contrary to its stated aim, the scheme has effectively rationed access to new technology rather than enhance it.

 **5**

The Special Aids to Employment scheme: an enabling force?

This chapter provides an exploration of the only statutory technology access measure for disabled workers in the United Kingdom. In the form of the Special Aids to Employment scheme (henceforward the SAE scheme), this measure can be seen to offer disabled workers access to otherwise disabling employment. It is noteworthy that the scheme receives little attention in the rehabilitation literature (Stevenson and Sutton 1983; Rajan 1985a; Cornes 1987, 1989, 1990; Murray and Kenny 1990), and where it is mentioned, it remains undertheorized (Ashok *et al.* 1985; Sandhu 1987; Carew and West 1989). This reflects the superficial treatment of new technology as an access tool for disabled people. Given the potential of the SAE scheme, its focus on 'special aids' to employment, one that fits well with a medical model interest in state-of-the-art technologies, it is remarkable that it should have received so little attention.

An analysis of the limited research on the efficacy of the SAE scheme (Snowdon Report 1980: 55; Topliss 1982; Employment Department 1989, 1990b; RADAR 1990a: 7–9, 1990b: 3–6, 1991: 25–6) would suggest that although benefiting a number of disabled workers, the SAE scheme has been based on deficit premises, and has seriously misrepresented the enabling potential of new technology for disabled people. This misrepresentation takes two main forms; firstly, that the scheme has been increasingly cost-driven, and that its functioning has been as much about excluding the 'un-deserving' as well as providing new technology. The Employment Service can be seen to have carefully avoided stating the numbers of unsuccessful applicants to the scheme (Employment Department 1990b). It will be argued that the scheme has limited the extent of specialized technology use by the rationing techniques it adopts. Secondly, by framing technological aids increasingly in terms of 'special aids' (that is, specialized devices) the scheme substantially underestimated the enabling potential of mainstream technology for disabled workers.

The chapter begins by taking a brief look at the historical development of the SAE scheme post-1944. This places the scheme into the wider policy context. The second part of the chapter looks at the recent changes in the provision of new technologies to disabled workers under the 1994 Access to Work (ATW) programme. Although the ATW programme became effective after this research was completed, and therefore did not shape the experiences of those researched, the future promise and problems of the programme, and its likely impact on disabled people, needs to be explored. The final part of the chapter argues that even the revisions to special aid provision wrought by the Access to Work measures do not address the essentially disablist premises of special aids provision. It argues that the deficit model adopted, and the absence of disabled people from the construction, working and review of these provisions, perpetuates disabling policy and provision.

The Special Aids to Employment scheme in a policy context

The SAE scheme was first established in 1944 under the Disabled Persons (Employment) Act of that year, legislation constructed under the aegis of the Tomlinson Committee (1942). The Act was a response to the urgent labour needs that followed the Second World War. The SAE represents one of a number of measures including the 3 per cent employment quota scheme, which attempted to enhance the employability of disabled men, many of whom were war-injured (for a broader discussion see Topliss 1982; Lonsdale 1986). These immediate post-war measures were from the outset a mixture of statutory and voluntary ideas, some being underpinned by legal redress, while others were based on encouragement and exhortation (Barnes 1991: 85). The SAE scheme fits squarely into the latter as it was based on the notion that employers and disabled employees apply for assistance from the scheme. No attempt was made to make the question of access to technology a statutory duty or right. A supply-side approach was adopted, one which conceptualized new technology as the corrective that would make a disabled person employable. Here, benefits were not seen to accrue from an altered workplace, nor enhanced demand per se, but from the repackaging of the individual to a work-ready capacity.

In theory, the Secretary of State was invested with the 'power' to provide special aids, adaptations and equipment to those disabled people deemed worthy of assistance. In practice, the administration of the scheme was entrusted to disablement resettlement officers, and later to the Disablement Advisory Service, which together in 1992 formed the Placement, Assessment and Counselling Teams, known as PACTs. Clearly, it was felt that the issue of access to technology was one that could be framed by employers and the Employment Service, occasionally in consultation with the person who was seeking assistance. While major changes have occurred in the operation of the 1944 Act with, for example, the diminished significance of the quota scheme (phased out in 1996), the SAE scheme remained remarkably similar in its basic aims and administration to that which was established in 1944 (Heppel 1992). The major changes have been in the kinds of special aids provided, the profile of the recipient group and the staffing of the scheme.

The kind of special aids provided were, during its early stages, a reflection of war injuries in providing aids for amputees and people with mobility impairments. Consequently, basic aids to mobility (sticks, crutches) were the main provision. During the 1940s, the meaning of 'special aids' can be seen as synonymous with state assistance to gain employment. In this way the term 'special' did not generally refer to the nature of the aids provided, but reflected the *special* nature of such interventions in the working of 1940s capitalism.

However modest the provisions of the early SAE, such an intervention in the employment relationship represented an important early symbol of a mixed economy of welfare and capitalist economics. However, it would be erroneous to assume that the scheme was rooted purely in humanitarian concerns, and it is worth restating that labour shortages were the main precipitant of the scheme, and that recent changes in the British labour market have made the efficacy of the scheme a less urgent question.

As new technology has become a cheaper, more ubiquitous feature of everyday life, it was inevitable that 'special aids' should begin to reflect this. By the 1980s the term 'special aids' had become synonymous with specialized technology; technology that is not ordinarily available in mainstream employment settings. The cost of the average provision has increased; indeed under the SAE there was no theoretical cost limit, save that (until 1994) any equipment over £3000 had to be sanctioned centrally by the Sheffield office of the Employment Service. As regards the profile of the special aids recipients, there is now a clear absence of war-related injuries that made up the earlier profile. Today the profile is made up of the major impairment 'types' affecting physical and sensory functions (see Harrison 1987: 30–1; Martin *et al.* 1988).

As regards the actual number getting assistance under the SAE scheme, the figure as at June 1992 stood at 5633 people (Heppel 1992). No figures are available for a comparison of numbers over the period 1944 to date; this is due in part to a failure by successive governments to review the scheme. However, this figure is remarkably low given the number of people who might have benefited. The low figure could be seen as a reflection of the low level of employment among disabled people (Martin, White and Meltzer 1989; Prescott-Clarke 1990; RNIB 1991). However, this alone cannot explain the very low levels of provision. The OPCS report of 1989 included figures of the numbers of disabled people in employment (Martin *et al.* 1989: 68–84). It discovered that of the 6.2 million disabled people in Britain, 2,452,800 are of working age, of which 760,368 are officially employed. If we assume, as the OPCS researchers do, that there is a significant number of disabled discouraged workers who are not employed, then it seems reasonable to argue that a figure of 5633 provisions for a possible employment population of 800,000 and above shows that in quantitative terms the scheme falls well short of its enabling potential. Even if we take the figures for the number of adult disabled people deemed by Martin *et al.* (1989) to have a severe disability (*sic*) and who are working (up to 65 years old), we can again see the likely gap between provision and enabling potential. The OPCS research by Martin *et al.* calculates as 92,715 all disabled people in severity categories 5–10 who are working. This is noteworthy, as we would expect this group to find technological aids of added value in their employment. The small numbers in receipt of special aids makes the question of the efficacy of the scheme, its basic premises and workings, an even more pressing concern. Previous reports on the SAE scheme hold some clues as to the small number of disabled people benefiting from the scheme. The Employment Department's *Evaluation of Special Schemes for People with Disabilities* (Employment Department 1990b) established that many of its special schemes had a very low profile, and that disabled applicants to the special schemes had first learnt about the scheme from friends or colleagues and not from the Employment Service's disablement resettlement officers or Disablement Advisory Service Staff (see also Employment Department 1989). This reliance on word-of-mouth awareness of the Employment Service's special schemes goes some way to explaining the low take-up of these provisions. Another explanation might be that a large number of applicants are refused assistance, and that significant numbers apply, but only a small percentage are successful. This latter point requires further examination and is addressed in this study.

Benefits of the SAE scheme

The most obvious benefit attributable to the scheme has been non-means-tested status, one designed to offer special aids to employment where a recipient is able to establish their needs as a disabled employee. While the notion of needs has rightly been criticized within disability studies (McKnight in Brechin *et al.* 1981; Oliver and Barnes in Bynoe *et al.* 1991) the SAE scheme grapples with the notion that provision should be made where employers are unable or unwilling to provide technological support for a disabled worker, regardless of their economic status.

By adopting a voluntaristic approach and thus avoiding compulsion, the scheme was seen to enhance employment opportunities and quality of working life while avoiding alienating employers. However, critics of the special schemes more generally see them as little more than a supply-side exercise in marketing disabled people to otherwise disablist employers:

> Their aim is to make individual disabled people suitable for work, but while they may succeed in individual cases, such programmes may also have the opposite effect. By packaging and selling them as a special case, the idea that there is something different about disabled people is reinforced.
>
> (Oliver in Brown and Scase 1991:138–9)

While Oliver's comments are important in demanding a broader reflection on the role of special schemes, in looking at the SAE it would be churlish to ignore its obvious benefits for some of its successful applicants. The open-ended nature of the SAE scheme and its rejection of an upper cash limit has been noteworthy. In a sense, this form of targeted funding seems to be an implicit trade-off that has been reached between numbers of identified recipients and the levels of support given under the scheme (Heppel 1992).

Limits of the SAE scheme

The obvious and immediate limitation of the SAE scheme is its restriction of beneficiaries to those whom it deems 'disabled' enough to warrant assistance. The result is that the Employment Service and their staff have been invested with the power to decide who will and who will not benefit from the scheme, based on a disabling eligibility test. This test looks not at the disabling employment barriers faced by an individual with an impairment, but at a (spurious) measure of bodily deficits alone. This amounts to a physical means-test which applicants have to satisfy in order to benefit from the scheme.

As regards who should benefit, the regulations of the scheme limited it to those in need of obvious and immediate assistance to do work that they otherwise would be unable to do because of a recognized 'disability' (impairment). Here the notion of disability is confused with impairment, while the perceived severity of a 'disability' (impairment) has been a key factor in the success or failure of the applicant. Thus, workers who are not severely or noticeably impaired risk falling outside of the remit of the scheme, regardless of the extent of disabling barriers they meet in their work. Here, the absence of a voice for the disabled applicant can be seen to compound the process of exclusion. The final decisions on 'disability' and 'severity' have been made by disablement resettlement officers or Disablement Advisory Service staff (Placement, Assessment and Counselling Teams from 1992). As no official records have been kept of the profile of rejections, this study will provide some insights into the decision-making process adopted by Employment Service staff.

An important limitation of the scheme, again one that relates to early assessment processes, is that the provision of technology can only be made where the technology is not otherwise available. That is, if the technology requested was deemed to be the employer's usual provision (for example if a standard PC is requested where the employer already uses them) then no provision has generally been made. This does not mean there is a refusal to provide mainstream technology, but there *is* a refusal to investigate whether or not the disabled worker has or is likely to have access to the technology in question. The danger here is that the disabled person may find themselves between an intransigent employer and a reluctant Employment Service official.

Another weakness of the SAE scheme is that equipment is on loan to a particular employment and is not the property of the disabled worker. This could discourage disabled workers from changing employments if they believed that it might jeopardize their access to technological aids.

Access to the SAE scheme

Until 1994, only those either in work or about to take up work have been allowed to benefit from the SAE scheme. There has been then the potential for a Catch-22 situation, one where applicants cannot receive help because they are not in or about to get work; but they are unable to get work because they cannot get the technological support they need. This applies particularly to job seekers with severe impairments who have usually had some experience of new technology, mainstream and/or specialized, and who know that without new technology their work would be very difficult. The regulations of the SAE scheme read in a way that is off-putting to those who do not have the chance of immediate employment. Relatedly, only those with permanent and stable work are likely to receive support, especially where expensive equipment is sought. An example of this stance is that although people in temporary and part-time work can receive assistance, the scope for provision and the likelihood of support are much diminished. Such a bias towards helping full-time permanent workers has been a feature of Employment Service measures. The growth of part-time and temporary work, however, has begun to receive ministerial attention (Department of Social Security 1990).

Another highly anomalous feature of the SAE scheme has been its requirement that only registered disabled people could benefit from the scheme. On the surface this seemed to make sense, given the need to identify suitable applicants. Curiously though, the requirement goes hand in hand with the actual collapse of the registration scheme, with less people joining the list of registered green card holders (Prescott-Clarke 1990; RADAR 1990b: 4–5; Glendinning 1991). Research also suggests that disabled people's knowledge of the green card registration scheme has been low, with recent Social and Community Planning Research findings pointing to a figure of 50 per cent of respondents not knowing the existence of the registration scheme (Prescott-Clarke 1990). Recent changes wrought by the Access to Work Programme have attempted to rectify this problem (see below).

A major problem is that the SAE scheme has been more likely to benefit those disabled workers in full-time, permanent contracts. The growth of casual or poor work (Pahl 1984; Oliver in Brown and Scase 1991: 132–46) may have further distanced disabled workers from the benefits of the SAE scheme. Here, ironically, there is scope for some disabled workers who are lucky enough to be in the 'core' of full-time permanent employment, to be the workers most likely to get technological support.

SAE provision and the communication of attitudes

The dearth of evidence available on the working of the SAE scheme at a national level suggests that the findings of this study will provide some useful evidence on the workings of the SAE and its successor scheme. To date most appraisals of the SAE have been subsumed under more general reviews of the Employment Service's Special Schemes, reviews instigated and re-searched by the Employment Service or its research agents (Employment Department 1989, 1990b). This form of self-review should be treated with some degree of critical scrutiny. However, the Employment Service's own reviews are a telling example of the weaknesses of the special schemes and the staff that operate them. An Employment Service study in 1989 described the civil servants who operate special schemes as having jobs, that in broad terms, are perceived to be low-status and unglamorous, and that

> Work with disabled people is given little status and even less priority in the employment service. Traditionally a low key operation, the stimulus provided by the introduction of DAS has long since dissipated. DROs and DAS are seen as operating away from the mainstream, even to the extent of physical isolation.
>
> (Employment Department 1989)

The report goes on to mention how few disablement resettlement officers and Disablement Advisory Service received support from senior manage-ment regarding the quality and value of their work.

As evidence of the low profile of the DRO/DAS workforce, of those who sought assistance through the pre-1994 special schemes, twice the number of beneficiaries actually received help from generalist job centre workers rather than from 'specialist' DRO and DAS staff (RADAR 1990b: 8).

A combination of poorly trained staff and the disabling premises of the SAE scheme has severely limited the enabling potential of the scheme. How-ever, Britain is not unique. The work of Al Cavalier (in Gartner and Joe 1987: 129–41) on the provision of technological support in the United States high-lights the disabling features of US technology facilitation schemes. Cavalier identifies three key disabling features of the schemes:

- where the primary focus is on the technology provided
- where the needs of the provider override those of the applicant; and
- where the provider focuses on the disability rather than the abilities of the recipient.

A theoretical critique of the SAE scheme: disabling premises

While the above has attempted to identify those factors likely to shape the day-to-day operation of the SAE scheme, a more important task is that of deconstructing the premises or basic assumptions behind the SAE scheme.

These premises can be seen to have placed a cultural boundary around both the working of the scheme and the broader question of the role of new technology in the lives of disabled workers.

The central assumption behind the SAE scheme is that it provides 'special' employment aids for disabled workers in order to correct or augment a physical deficit *they* have. The assumption is that the disabled person is the problem being ameliorated, and not social and attitude barriers; this in turn has led to the requirement that a disabled applicant should have to establish their eligibility for special aids by emphasizing the severity of their 'disability' (impairment). This not only ignores the broader social factors that might lead the applicant to ask for assistance, but also places the onus on disabled applicants to prove their eligibility.

An alternative way to view the process of providing aids, equipment and adaptations would be to refocus attention on the broader factors that lead to the request for assistance. This would involve looking at the employment environment to discover what interventions would allow for a reduction of the barriers that may limit a disabled person's working ability. Also, an enabling scheme would place the onus on the employer and/or the state to make working environments accessible. Here then the fundamental difference between a *deficit* and a *barriers* approach is that the latter focuses on the actual limits in the physical and social environment of the disabled person. In practical terms this would translate into a rights-based scheme. To what extent have recent changes led to a more enabling provision of technological support for disabled people?

Access to Work and beyond

From June 1994, the SAE scheme has been subsumed within the new Access to Work (ATW) initiative. This change reflects the government's awareness of the limits of previous special schemes, particularly the limited numbers benefiting from the schemes, and the delays and inflexibilities in SAE and Adaptations to Premises (APE) provisions (Employment Department 1989, 1990b; RADAR 1991: 25–6; *Disability Now* 1993: 1–9). These changes, announced by the then Employment Secretary David Hunt in July 1993, were said to offer a more flexible package of access provisions, with an expanded budget and employer contributions of 50 per cent of the costs of aids and assistance, providing an increased and wider range of provision (RADAR 1993a: 7, 1993b: 3).

A major aim of the ATW reforms was to ensure that more disabled people were to benefit from the scheme. An example of this wider provision was the announcement of a personal assistance scheme for disabled workers – an acknowledgement that employment and personal assistance are not mutually exclusive. Despite these changes, criticism rained down on the government changes, with strident condemnation from the mainstream disability organizations (RADAR, RNIB) and employer organizations (notably the

Confederation of British Industry) (in RADAR 1993c: 4). Susan Scott-Parker of the Employers' Forum on Disability summed up the general response to employer contributions in stating: 'Any measure that discourages employers from developing positive policies on retention of disabled employees is very worrying' (in *Disability Now* 1993: 9). Perhaps this response from employers was not surprising, given the reluctance of many employers to incur costs for special aids and adaptations. This rejection of key features of the ATW programme by employers can be seen as symbolic of the difficulties the changes threatened, the ultimate loser being the disabled applicant seeking support to enter or stay in an increasingly competitive and hostile employment environment. Caroline Gooding, policy officer at the RADAR, captured this image of disabled people being squeezed by the advent of the ATW:

> Many employers will not be prepared to pay extra money to retain staff. At a time when the official unemployment rate for disabled people is 19 per cent and there is an enormous pool of hidden unemployment, what is needed is more not less government assistance
>
> (in *Disability Now* 1993: 1)

By the time the ATW initiative was introduced in June 1994 the government had already bowed to the pressure of the weight of criticism and had withdrawn the requirement of employers to contribute to special assistance provision (but see Beinart *et al.* 1996 for evidence that, informally, PACT staff were encouraging employers to contribute during this period) and Employment Secretary David Hunt promised an extra £2 million to increase the number of beneficiaries of the scheme. The ATW did have a wider remit than the previous special schemes, with unemployed and self-employed disabled people being included for the first time as potential applicants. To benefit from ATW applicants had no longer to be registered, but had to be 'registrable'. While this signified the acknowledged decline of the disabled persons register, the requirement to be registrable means that applicants still face a physical means-test rooted firmly within a deficit model, and demands that applicants establish their eligibility to ATW provision. A worrying aspect of the shift to ATW, with its emphasis on aiding more disabled people, was the establishment of an upper limit of £21,000 of provision over a five-year period. This was seen as potentially deleterious to applicants with visual impairments or severe physical impairments, in the sense that it symbolized the increasingly cost-driven nature of the ATW at the expense of a more demand-led approach. The government did, however, offer an assurance that the £21,000 limit could be exceeded in 'exceptional circumstances' where applicants established that their request is necessary and reasonable (RADAR 1994: 1–2). This stipulation seems odd given that the request for support of more than £21,000 is very uncommon, and is likely to represent a package of support for someone who clearly requires significant ATW provision (Beinart *et al.* 1996: 89).

By the autumn of 1995, eighteen months after the launch of the ATW, evidence of the severe rationing of the scheme was already surfacing. This began to question the efficacy of the scheme, its ability to provide both a breadth of coverage and a meaningful depth of provision. Evidence of the refusal to provide technological support for a blind applicant to ATW, and of special equipment taking six months to arrive were reported (*Disability Now* 1995a: 1–2). These details suggested that all was not well with the operation of the ATW scheme. At the same time the Employment Secretary announced a review of the ATW scheme as it was growing too rapidly, and was £2 million over budget for the year 1995/6. While there is evidence to support the growth of ATW spending, with a 1995/6 budget of £13.4 million (the schemes had cost £3.5 million in the year 1994/5), this overspend was exploited by ministers who argued that employers must begin to contribute to the scheme's growth. In December 1995, the Employment Service wrote to all large beneficiary organizations asking if they would be prepared to contribute to the funding of future provision. This highlights the contingent nature of the scheme's provisions, and the risks to potential beneficiaries at times of economic downturn (*Disability Now* 1995b: 5).

A manifestation of the new rationing of the ATW scheme was the announcement by Gillian Shephard, the Education Secretary in the newly combined Department for Education and Employment, that the scheme would henceforth be targeted on unemployed applicants and existing beneficiaries of ATW (in *Disability Now* 1996a: 4, 1996b: 1–2). While the emphasis on unemployed applicants is laudable, the government's awareness that historically applications had come primarily from those in employment may seem to represent a cynical manoeuvre. For example, the recent Social and Community Planning Research review of the ATW programme suggests that 95 per cent of all ATW applications during the June 1994 to June 1995 period were from employed and self-employed applicants (Beinart *et al.* 1996: 25). This begs the serious question as to the motivations behind this move. Was the move purely a smokescreen for a freezing of the budget in the knowledge that unemployed applicants are a small proportion of all ATW applicants?

The commitment to existing beneficiaries of the ATW scheme was itself placed in doubt with the publication in March 1996 of more evidence of refusals to fund adequately the ATW programme (*Disability Now* 1996b: 1–2). It seemed clear by the middle of 1996 that the government could not afford to meet the weight of applications that had now been lodged for ATW provision.

The increase of ATW funding to £19 million in the financial year 1996/7 provides evidence of the government's attempts to keep up with rising demand for the ATW scheme. This growth in the numbers applying to the ATW programme seems fairly clear evidence of a catching-up exercise, where disabled applicants formerly refused help or unaware of special scheme help, begin to claim their rights to access in employment environments. Unfortunately, the contribution of employers was established firmly in May 1996 in order to honour a 'commitment to existing beneficiaries' requiring additional or renewed support. A complex formula was established, employers having to pay the first £300 of provision and 20 per cent of costs above that up to

£10,000 over three years. Any provision above that would be met by ATW funds. This is interesting as the percentage receiving provision of £10,000 and above was only 8 per cent of all applicants. Forty-eight per cent of all applications received less than £1000. This is evidence not only that ATW fails to meet disabled people's aggregate employment needs, but also evidence of the inconsistent workings of the scheme. This inconsistency is borne out in the government's own recent survey of the ATW programme (Beinart *et al.* 1996).

The 1996 survey of the ATW scheme (Beinart *et al.* 1996) provided a review of the scheme's operation and effectiveness in its first 12 months. The findings suggest obvious improvements over the former special schemes: a larger number of beneficiaries and a more inclusive construction of eligible applicants. However, the framing of the review and the questions addressed fall far short of a critical review, indeed the report seems more concerned with costing the scheme and monitoring the 'wastage' of the scheme than measuring its effectiveness for disabled people. The first weakness of the review is that it excludes the experiences of those disabled applicants who were refused assistance. This is a grave oversight. It needs to be acknowledged that the official rejection rate of 10 per cent hides a number of applicants whose applications were never processed and whose attempts were scotched during preliminary telephone enquiries.

The exact number of rejections in the geographical areas covered by PACTs suggest a large variation in the level of official rejections, as the survey accepts:'The number of rejected applications ranged from 0–44' (Beinart *et al.* 1996: 88). This is a startling figure given that most PACTs had under 70 applications during the period surveyed, with an average (mean) application figure of 42. According to the researchers:'This variation in the number of rejected applications could be due to the different ways in which PACTs categorize and record rejections' (Beinart *et al.* 1996: 88). This lends support to the notion that calculations of the number of rejections are spurious in research terms, as each PACT was allowed to measure these rejections in whichever way it saw fit. Given the political struggle over the ATW scheme and the fierce lobbying by its critics, this anomaly is hardly surprising. It is convenient that no definitive measure of rejections is possible at this stage. Similarly, no national register is kept of ATW recipients, the SCPR research team being dependent on the collated registers of the individual PACTs surveyed.

It is not surprising, given the careful selection of interviewees for the survey, that the level of reported satisfaction with the ATW scheme was high. However, the significant expansion in beneficiaries, and the obvious improvement in reported delivery time of provisions, were evidence of the obvious benefits of the revised programme. It is also noteworthy that 82 per cent of the successful applicants to ATW had applied for and received 'Special Aids and Equipment'. Although the 1996 survey makes it difficult to disaggregate these special aids, a rough calculation would suggest that about 50 per cent are in the form of new technology, with the remainder being posture and mobility aids. This highlights the importance of the ATW programme in creating enabling environments, and makes a critical review of the programme a pressing issue.

A careful reading of the survey provides some worrying anomalies which might suggest a number of invalid or at least spurious findings. For example, there are vast discrepancies between the answers given to a question which asked 'Were you asked to make a contribution [to the cost of provision]'. Only 10 per cent of employers said they had been asked to contribute, as opposed to 59 per cent of disability employment advisers (DEAs) saying they asked employers for a contribution (Beinart *et al.* 1996: 158). This is again evidence of inconsistencies in the working of the ATW programme. Also the degree of satisfaction with the ATW programme – with 91 per cent of ATW recipients being either fairly satisfied or very satisfied – seems interesting, given that the same Employment Service personnel who staffed the pre-1994 special schemes are also likely to be delivering the ATW programme. Evidence shows that the average length of time DEAs had been in post was five years. This suggests that the majority of DEAs will have worked with the former special schemes and experienced the low status and poor training that work involved (Employment Department 1989, 1990b). In all, 44 per cent had been in disability-related work for five or more years. Can we believe that the cultural changes that have come about with ATW have really changed the style and efficacy of delivery as much as the SCPR survey suggests?

These points should caution readers against a too-literal reading of the survey, as the political objectives of the PACT staff – especially considering the close scrutiny of the ATW programme by the Department for Education and Employment – clearly may have served to contaminate some of the survey findings. There is no question that the administration of the ATW programme has to date been a delicate exercise, given the politicized treatment of the programme.

Although this programme became effective after the empirical research for this book was completed, the above findings help build a model of the likely trajectory of government support for 'special aids' in the next ten years. Having acknowledged some clear benefits that accrue from the ATW programme, it is important to restate that the ATW programme is still firmly rooted in a deficit model of disability, and is a programme which has not been designed, framed, or reviewed by disabled people. In this sense, the scheme retains a number of key similarities with the earlier Special Aids to Employment and allied schemes. Firstly, eligibility is still decided by PACT 'experts'. Secondly, the definition of disability implicit in the working of the scheme is itself disabling; at one point the survey asked respondents to detail 'the effect of disability on working life' (Beinart *et al.* 1996: 17). This in turn fails to connect aids and equipment with a redefinition of the workplace, but instead sees their role as one of correcting the ailing body. Additionally these questions are unnecessarily negative and demoralizing. In this way no account is taken of a disabling employment environment. Employers once again escape the scrutiny they deserve in the assessment of the benefits of special aids.

Here the refusal by employers to fund is not connected to disabling environments, but is seen as a rational business decision which recognizes the cost of the disabled person's deficits to the organization – costs which the state should meet.

Finally, the problematizing of the growth of the ATW programme is one of the most shocking features of the changes made since June 1994. The discourse around the scheme – it has been described as the victim of its own success (the extent of this success remains questionable) – and the governmental portrayal of the scheme as too costly is a highly negative development. The cultural boundary has been firmly recast around the ATW programme: it has been portrayed as accruing high per capita costs, and as a luxury the state can ill afford. A parallel discourse surrounds the desire to spread the benefits of special aid schemes to a wider constituency, thus justifying cost limits and employer contributions. This is a clever ploy, as it legitimates retrograde measures in the name of widening access by arguing that more can benefit only if reductions are made in support to current beneficiaries. Clearly the broadening of beneficiaries of special schemes is exactly what disabled people want and are beginning to demand. However, the hegemonic construction of this question as a zero sum game is highly specious but politically effective (see Gillian Shephard's remarks in *Disability Now* 1996a: 4).

Conclusion

This chapter has appraised the state-led provision of special aids and equipment to disabled people. It has been argued that both the SAE scheme and ATW not only fail to meet the needs of disabled people on a day-to-day basis, but that they are fundamentally flawed by disabling premises. These premises, in line with other policy measures for disabled people, have closed off a wider discussion of enabling policies by establishing a cultural or hegemonic boundary around the question of disabled people's new technology 'needs' and how they are met. The disabling premises of the scheme suggest that administrative changes to the basic scheme will not overcome the limitations of the scheme, as the ATW developments confirm. The development of enabling policies in the field of new technology support demands policies with explicitly enabling premises, ones constructed from the expressed ideas of disabled people themselves.

This chapter brings to a close the background theoretical exploration of the potential benefits of new technology and those factors likely to facilitate or limit these benefits. It is an appropriate point at which to begin to look at the findings of the national research that constitutes the core of this work.

 # PART 2

THE EXPERIENCE OF DISABLED WORKERS USING NEW TECHNOLOGY

 **6**

Disabled workers and new technology

Having looked at the limits and problems of deficit model studies of disabled workers using new technology, the research findings of this study will now be delineated. The results suggest that new technology is significant in addressing the barriers disabled workers face, while also affirming the value of a social barriers model of the 'disability problem' in employment settings. This supports a social barriers perspective in suggesting that it is attitude, environmental and technical barriers that have limited disabled people at work, and that new technology is significant primarily in its potential to challenge these barriers. The findings provide a strong counter to deficit model research, which continues to frame the benefits of new technology in terms of its correction of disabled people. Unfortunately, the findings also suggest that new technology does not erase these barriers entirely, and that these barriers continue to limit some disabled workers' daily experiences.

This chapter provides a profile of disabled people using new technology in their work, and is based on findings of the first stage of this study, a self-completion questionnaire completed by a national sample of 78 disabled people who work/ed with new technology. These findings give an overall impression of disabled people's employment experiences with new technology. These provide a backcloth against which the more detailed qualitative findings of Stage 2 of the study can be understood.

In order to obtain a national picture of disabled workers using new technology we need to begin the process of profiling responses. Such a profile will not only provide a comprehensive image of disabled technology users, it will also indicate if some disabled people have gained more than others. The findings also provide insights as to:

- the extent disabled workers use new technology in their work;
- how many participants had used new technology in their work but were now unemployed;

- to what extent specialized new technology was being used by disabled workers.

A profile of disabled workers using new technology

Sex and age groupings

It seems clear that disabled workers using new technology and finding it significant in their work are more likely to be men. In all, 24 respondents were women and 54 were men. This represented a percentage split of 31 per cent women and 69 per cent men. This may suggest that disabled women are less likely to be using new technology in their employment; alternatively it may also be a measure of differential gender perceptions of skill and employment, with women less likely to see their work as significant generally. However, the latter argument may seem rather outdated, with women's increased representation in paid employment and professional careers. This sex discrepancy requires further research, but at first sight the substantial difference by sex is worrying given that women represent the vast majority of workers in clerical and intermediate white-collar employments (Phillips and Taylor 1980; Purcell *et al.* 1986). This fact applies equally to disabled women workers (Prescott-Clarke 1990). This also has implications for the research, as it suggests that the findings and policy implications may be skewed towards the experiences of a predominantly male population. The wider social implications may be that disabled women may not benefit fully from technological change, and also that the perception of technology as an adjunct to the enabling process may be recognized more fully by disabled men.

The age range of participants conforms to those established at the outset as 16–64, with the majority of participants in the 35–44 (36 per cent) and 45–54 (30 per cent) age groups (Table 6.1). The small number of participants in the 16–24 age group (6 per cent) is worrying, as it seems to fly in the face of expectations about youth and computer literacy. However, the greater propensity for young people to be without work may help explain this relative dearth of young disabled participants (Ashton and Maguire 1986; Clark and Hirst 1989). The exact reasons for this small percentage representation is difficult to establish in research of this kind; however, the experiences of the

Table 6.1   *Age distribution of disabled workers (base = 78)*

Age distribution	Percentage	(Number)
16–24	6	(5)
25–34	22	(17)
35–44	36	(28)
45–54	30	(23)
55–64	6	(5)

younger participants will subsequently be viewed with this low representation in mind.

Of interest is data garnered for the Social and Community Planning Research study *Employment and Handicap,* which suggests that disabled 16- to 24-year-olds represent 12 per cent of all disabled employees in Great Britain (Prescott-Clarke 1990: 94) and 2–3 per cent of the total population of disabled people (Martin *et al.* 1988: 27). This suggests young disabled people may not be realizing the full potential of new technology in their employment. However, it is worth remembering that the 25–34 age group represents 22 per cent of the overall participants, which provides some promise for those currently in the 16–24 age group. Finally the age group 55–64 accounts for only 6 per cent of the main sample. This is more easily explained in terms of the greater likelihood of both disabled men and women withdrawing from employment prior to their fiftieth birthday (Martin *et al.* 1989: 71).

New technology and employment type

For the purposes of this study, employment type was distinguished in two ways: firstly, in terms of the actual employment performed, and secondly, whether the participant was a computer worker or a technology user. As regards the type of employment disabled people were doing, the findings suggest a broad range of work: junior clerical workers, computer-aided designers, telephonists, programmers, administrators, computer analysts, analytical chemists and computer-based authors.

The distinction between computer workers and technology users was adopted because it was felt that computer work might provide qualitatively different employment to technology use. Here computer workers (analysts, programmers, hardware and software engineers) were seen as existing because of the development of the microchip technology. It was also felt that because of its recent genesis, the employment culture of computing may present unique opportunities (and conceivably barriers) for disabled workers, in that established employment divisions and structures might be absent. Conversely, technology users were seen to be those workers who used technology to do a job that would, at one time, have been performed by other means, for example clerical work, filing, manual typing, manual chemical analysis. It was felt that the level of time spent with technology might vary much more than in computer work.

Of the 78 disabled people surveyed, 67 per cent (52) were technology users, while 33 per cent (26) were employed in a variety of computer work. A breakdown of these workers by sex shows that women are more likely to be found in the technology user category, with 79 per cent of women in this category as against 60 per cent of men. Conversely, in the computer worker category men predominate, with 40 per cent of all men and 21 per cent of all women in this category. This sex profile should be borne in mind in any conclusions made, if any, about the differential experiences of computer workers and technology users.

Education and training

The levels of education and training again vary widely; however, the overall impression is of a higher than expected level of education, but of a dearth of formal training among the disabled participants. In terms of education, the profile of 78 provides a massive figure of 61 per cent (48) who had attained A level and above qualifications. Of the remainder, 25 per cent (20) had obtained O level, and 14 per cent (10) less than O level or no formal education. The educational profile of the disabled participants was notable, as highest levels of education exceed significantly the education levels of the general population (Table 6.2). Here the 1980 *General Household Survey* provided a figure of all those economically active individuals, aged 25–69 years, who attained an educational level of A level and above as 20 per cent. Although like is not being compared with like, as the former are new-technology-inclusive workers, it is reasonable to assert that the disabled participants had a higher than average level of education than their non-disabled counterparts. This credential anomaly is not unique in disability research. The study by Prescott-Clarke (1990) on *Disability and Employment* established that the number of disabled workers with A level and above qualifications (28 per cent) was higher than for the general population. However, the research also established that 42 per cent of disabled workers had no formal education (Prescott-Clarke 1990: 94; see also Martin *et al.* 1989: 72, for a similar educational profile). This contrasts sharply with the above findings.

In their study of remote homeworkers using new technology, Ashok *et al.* (1985) found that their sample of participants were overqualified for their work relative to able-bodied workers doing the same activity. Ashok concluded that disabled people, as with other minority groups, had to obtain better than average education in order to secure average jobs (Ashok *et al.* 1985; see also Graham *et al.* 1990: 7–8. On the educational differentials of black and white job applicants see Brown and Gay 1985). However, it should be remembered that there were 26 computer workers in the research, for whom degree level education is increasingly a prerequisite. Here too the sex profile of participants suggests differential educational achievements. While men had an even spread of educational achievement, women presented a more polarized set of educational achievements. Although the proportion of

Table 6.2   *Educational attainment of disabled workers (base = 78)*

Educational attainment	Percentage	(Number)
Degree	28	(22)
Above A level	14	(11)
A level or equivalent	19	(15)
O level or equivalent	25	(20)
CSE or equivalent	4	(3)
No formal education	2	(1)
Other	8	(6)

women holding a degree (33 per cent) was higher than men (26 per cent), there were also more women over the whole profile who had less than A level qualifications: 16 per cent of women as against 6 per cent of men. This polarity may also have implications if education is found to be an indicator of overall success and satisfaction in employment with new technology.

An important accompaniment to educational attainment is that of training. Here an analysis of experiences suggests that while the quantitative level of both general and specific training were high, with 77 per cent and 83 per cent respectively receiving training. The perceived quality of training was low in many instances and inadequate in others. Much of the training, where detailed, was of an in-house or on-the-job type. This for many participants led to inferior and ad hoc training programmes. This mirrors national disquiet about the quality of new technology training for all workers (Rajan 1985b). However, the result of poor training may have particular significance for disabled workers.

Alongside job-specific training, questions were asked about the disabled participants' experiences (if any) of medical and employment rehabilitation. Rehabilitation was a focus of attention as it had surfaced as a feature of the pre-employment experiences of some of the disabled people involved in the pilot stage of the study. It transpired that only a minority had experienced rehabilitation, with 13 per cent and 19 per cent having medical and employment rehabilitation respectively. However small, the significance of rehabilitation was seen as an important facet of disabled people's experiences and biography. Clearly, the presence or absence of new technology in rehabilitation settings was raised as an important question at this stage.

Socio-economic profile

A good way to obtain a profile of the employment status and likely conditions of the 78 disabled participants was to apply accepted socio-economic groups (SEGs) to their employment. Again the results reflect findings on educational attainment, namely that the sample are more likely to be in professional and managerial work than disabled workers more generally and the employed population nationally. For example, the professional and managerial categories constitute 52 per cent (41) of the total 78 sample, a massive figure compared to the figure for economically active disabled workers more generally. A comparison can be gleaned from the recent Social and Community Planning Research which suggests a figure of 12 per cent of disabled workers in professional and managerial employment (Prescott-Clarke 1990: 94). A very similar figure of 18 per cent of all disabled workers being in the professional or managerial socio-economic group was established in recent OPCS research (Martin *et al.* 1989: 81).

The high number of disabled workers in professional or managerial work requires further analysis, but at this stage the increasing expectation that computer workers should hold degree level education, and the perception of analyst and programmer work as professional, both give clues but not definitive explanations as to the heavy weighting of professional and managerial workers in the sample. (On the process of professionalization see Johnson 1972; Pettigrew 1975; Freidson 1986; MacDonald 1995.)

Employment sectors

Other evidence on the profile of disabled workers using new technology can be identified in the findings on employment sector and size of establishment. The majority of workers in the study worked in public sector organizations. Here, 60 per cent (47) worked with new technology in a variety of public sector jobs, from newly established civil service agencies, through nuclear research establishments to general hospitals. Unemployed participants were categorized in terms of their last employment.

A number of participants worked in the public sector providing a service for other disabled people. The second largest sector were those workers employed in private organizations. Here a total of 28 per cent (22) worked in such organizations, again in a range of employments. The remaining 12 per cent (9) were self-employed. Of significance was the detail that all self-employed participants had at some point been employees, and most had their first experiences of new technology in paid employment. This figure of 12 per cent is representative of the increasing number of ex-employees entering self-employment (Spilsbury 1986). It is noteworthy that self-employment is rarely mentioned in research on disability and employment. It is also worth reflecting at this stage as to whether self-employment itself is made more accessible by new-technology-inclusive work.

The concentration of the majority of participants in the public sector might suggest that this is due to a long-standing ideological commitment of public sector employers to greater quota fulfilment, and their more system-atized personnel policies. This is a useful if limited explanation, one which may be broadly correct, but which obscures the huge variation in public sector quota fulfilment (Employment Department 1990c, 1990d). Another, perhaps more convincing explanation, is that public sector employment is notably large-scale. The National Health Service employs approximately one million workers alone and is the largest employer in western Europe. Equally, employment in the National Health Service is highly polarized, with an increased number of deregulated and low paid jobs (Fevre in Brown and Scase 1991: 67). Perhaps there is greater likelihood of technological presence in larger organizations (Daniel 1987). Although the public sector has been slower in adopting new technology relative to the private sector, the recent growth in new technology use in large public sector organizations cannot be overestimated.

It is clear from the research that the majority of disabled people working with new technology work in large (100 plus), mainly public sector organiza-tions, with 70 per cent of public employees working in such settings. Small and medium organizations were less commonly represented, with 7 per cent and 14 per cent of organizations respectively. The self-employed accounted for 9 per cent of participant responses; this is less than the actual figure who are self-employed, as one respondent preferred to be placed into the category of small organization.

Impairment type

Although not placing primacy on impairment type, a brief examination of these data was felt necessary, and would help illuminate the nuanced relationship between impairment type, the experience of new technology and the perception of employment barriers. The most numerous impairment group was that of musculo-skeletal difficulties (Table 6.3). Here some 27 per cent (21) of participants belonged to this category. The remaining 73 per cent (57) was made up of a range of impairments. However, within this range, it is worth noting that together visual impairments, congenital impairments, paraplegia, hemiplegia and tetraplegia constituted 47 per cent of the remaining participants.

These figures broadly reflect the findings of the distribution of impairments noted in an OPCS study of disabled people (Martin *et al.* 1988: 34). Martin and colleagues had found musculo-skeletal 'disabilities' to be the commonest overall grouping. However, the OPCS figures differ markedly in terms of neurological and ear impairments, which feature much less in this research and more prominently in the OPCS findings. While differential data gathering, classificatory methods and research populations differ, the overlap in the data suggests a measure of representativeness among the research sample. For the purposes of this study, they also provide potentially diverse experiences, with severe sensory impairments, a range of mobility impairments and dexterity impairments all featuring in the study.

Up to this point Stage 1 of the research paints a general picture of the broad characteristics of disabled technology workers: typically they are employed in a large public sector organization over a range of employments with new technology, and have a higher than expected educational profile. However, these details hide a number of important subtleties that require examination. The first important caveat is that of the 78 who can all be described as economically active, only 81 per cent (63) were employed on a full-time

Table 6.3   *Impairment classification (base = 78)*

Impairment classification	Percentage	(Number)
Musculo-skeletal	27	(21)
Auditory	5	(4)
Visual	17	(13)
Neurological	9	(7)
Congenital	15	(12)
Plegias	15	(12)
Other	12	(9)

basis. Of the remainder 8 per cent (6) worked part-time, 10 per cent (8) were unemployed but seeking work, and one participant was on sick leave. All of the unemployed participants had at some point worked with new technology.

How much technology was used?

The extent to which new technology forms an integral part of the lives of disabled workers is itself a measure of the legitimacy or otherwise of this research. If we attempt to measure the impact of new technology on disabled workers, it is important to establish that the extent of use is substantial enough to warrant attention. All participants felt that new technology was significant, thus providing clues as to its quantitative significance. The results bear this out; while 31 per cent (24) of participants used one or two technologies, 69 per cent (54) of participants used three or more forms of technology in their everyday work (Table 6.4). These data seem to be 'shadow' data for technology users and computer workers respectively. This reflects the greater variety of technology and applications most computer workers use. However, for most workers new technology was used in a variety of forms.

An example of a user of more than three technologies took the form of a programmer with a severe visual impairment using a document scanner to input text, an enlarged screen and software package, and Braille output devices to check printed documents. Additionally, the programmer made use of e-mail, facsimile machines and a large key 'notetaker' used in meetings. Another measure of the quantitative significance of technology was to ask the participants to estimate their percentage use of new technology as a proportion of their normal working week. The figures support the notion that use is substantial, with 78 per cent (61) of participants using new technology for at least 50 per cent of their working week. Only 11 per cent (9) of participants used new technology for less than 25 per cent of their working week.

The nature and origin of the technology used

The media image of new technology as dramatic interventions (Karpf 1988: 153–61), as 'high' technology and 'state-of-the-art' equipment, may suggest to the reader the image of many disabled workers using such technology to enable them to enter and participate in the working world. While the previous example suggests that this is sometimes the case, the overall findings

Table 6.4   *Number of technologies used (base = 78)*

Number of technologies* used	Percentage	(Number)
1 or 2	31	(24)
3 or more	69	(54)

*Hardware, but includes e-mail as this application was very significant in piloting

suggest that most commonly workers use mainstream technology. In all, 72 per cent of participants (56) used off-the-peg mainstream hardware and software, 17 per cent (13) had made minor adaptations such as extra support of the keyboard, or the removal of the rubber feet from the keyboard to allow extra manoeuvrability. In only 11 per cent (9) of instances had specially designed or adapted technology been used (Table 6.5).

The use of specialized hardware and software applications was sometimes in conjunction with mainstream personal computers. An interesting detail to come out of the findings was that two of the participants who used mainstream technology stated that they used their mainstream personal computer in a 'normal' way, in this instance with their feet. This suggests that it is not simply the type of technology that is important in assessing the kind of work disabled new technology users do.

These findings support one of the main tenets of this research: the need to avoid undue emphasis on dramatic interventions and eye-catching case studies which misrepresent the commonest experiences. Another possible inference is that those requiring specialized technology as a means of access to employment may not be receiving it. A latent workforce may exist – one stymied by the very agencies established to provide special aids to employment. This needs to be explored further.

An examination of the source of new technology suggests that most participants worked with new technology provided by their employers. Of the 78 participants, 69 per cent (54) were using technology provided by their employer, while a surprisingly large figure of 14 per cent (11) were using new technology provided by themselves or by charities (Table 6.6). Of the 11 people using charity or self-funded technology, three were either unemployed or underemployed and were using new technology at home in the hope that they might eventually get more substantial employment.

In total, 17 per cent (13) of participants were using some form of specially provided new technology. In 8 per cent (6) of instances, the Disablement Advisory Service (now part of the PACT) was the sole providers of specialized technology. This reflects the DAS's role in aiming to provide what employers cannot normally be expected to provide. However, the DAS team were not averse to providing mainstream technology where it was part of a wider specialized package of support. The relative scarcity of workers using

Table 6.5   *Type of technology used (base = 78)*

Type of technology	Percentage	(Number)
Specially designed/adapted	9	(7)
Mainstream with minor adaptations	17	(13)
Mainstream	72	(56)
Mix of technology types*	2	(2)

*In this instance the workers used both mainstream and specialized technologies

Table 6.6   *Sources of new technology (base = 78)*

Source	Percentage	(Number)
Employer	69	(54)
Disablement Advisory Service	8	(6)
Self	6	(5)
Gift/Charity	8	(6)
Mix of sources	9	(7)

specialized technology could be put down to a number of factors that require further exploration.

Firstly, as stated earlier, it is possible that there is a pool of unmet aspirations which could be facilitated by specialized technology. Here, 'unmet aspirations' could refer to disabled people unable to get work; or they could be the unmet aims, and self-defined needs, of those in work. Alternatively, it could simply be that disabled people needing specialized technology actually represent a minority of users, and that no expansion of provision needs to be made. This issue will be explored in later chapters of this book. Also of importance is an exploration of the functioning of the former Disablement Advisory Service teams (up until 1994 this team was responsible for the frontline provision of special aids to employment) and their provisions of technology in support of disabled workers. The figure of 8 per cent (6) of workers receiving technological assistance from charitable sources is significant. This may suggest some ignorance of, or possibly unsuccessful applications to, the Employment Service's Special Aids to Employment scheme.

At-home support

This may seem a curious focus for research on disabled people's employment experience, where home is usually seen as the antithesis of work. However, the piloting process highlighted an important point for some disabled participants. Although homeworkers were included in the research and amount to 9 per cent of the 78 participants, a total of 35 per cent of all participants used technology at home in support of their employment. This is a surprising figure, one that may have some bearing on later analyses. Such home support can be placed into two categories. Firstly, there are workers who use technology as an extension of their normal day and do more of the same work, but at home. Some of these communicate with their workplace out of hours. Secondly, there are those workers who use technology at home to develop their abstract competencies with new technology; this was seen to be a response to the rapid changes in computing and software. Such home-based activity is not so much homework as personal skills development. A number of participants cited their struggle to get work commensurate with their abilities, and justified their underemployment as a reason for working at home in order to keep up with technological developments.

The small number of homeworkers who worked from home were mostly the self-employed, in contrast with the directly supervised and often routinized work setting of employees. This was seen as important given the potential of home-based work for greater personal autonomy for disabled workers. Any significant differences in experiences will be explored below. It is worth stating that the range of self-employment activities was wide. Most of the full-time home-based work could be described as professional in character. Notably, the small number of part-time home-based workers seemed to be less satisfied with their generally less secure and less well-rewarded work. The question of employment satisfaction was explored more generally in order to establish whether the advent of new technology had enhanced the overall satisfaction of disabled workers.

Satisfaction and disabled workers

Participants were asked if work was more satisfying with the advent of new technology, given their status as a disabled worker. The results were unambiguous, with 57 per cent (45) being more satisfied with their work after new technology was introduced. Only 7 per cent of workers (5) were less satisfied with their work with the introduction of new technology. The remaining 36 per cent (28) had experienced mixed or unchanged levels of satisfaction after the introduction of new technology (Table 6.7).

The mixed category is explicable in terms of a number of participants becoming disabled while working with new technology, by participants whose quality of working was tempered by the intensity of work with new technology, and, significantly, by unemployed participants, most of whom commented on their ambivalence towards new technology, seeing both its short-term effect in enhancing job satisfaction as well as its negative effect on employment in the long term.

Significantly a figure of 57 per cent of participants were more satisfied with their work after the advent of new technology. However, there was clear evidence that some disabled people felt new technology to be deleterious or a mixed blessing. Higher satisfaction levels were noted by computer workers as against technology users, and satisfaction also correlated with level of education. Variable analyses on the question of satisfaction suggested that the variables of age, sex and socio-economic status were not statistically significant in relation to satisfaction levels.

Table 6.7 *Impact of technology on worker satisfaction (base = 78)*

Impact on level of satisfaction	Percentage	(Number)
Less satisfied	7	(5)
More satisfied	57	(45)
Unchanged	18	(14)
Mixed impact	18	(14)

Perhaps the most interesting findings to emanate from the questionnaire were responses to questions on the benefits of new technology and the barriers to enabling technology use. Here 90 per cent of respondents cited particular benefits for them as disabled workers in overcoming workplace and employment barriers. However, this figure needs to be set alongside the figure of 81 per cent of respondents who felt that barriers remained to enabling employment. The complexities of these figures will be explored in subsequent chapters which explore benefits and barriers in more detail. The ease with which respondents answered barriers-style questions is also significant and provides evidence of the value and relevance of a social barriers model in researching disabled people's lives.

Conclusion

This chapter has provided details of the characteristics of a national sample of 78 disabled people who work or have worked with new technology. We can begin to see how respondents do not conform to the picture presented in deficit model research. It is this national image of new technology workers that provides the context for the exploration of the qualitative experience of new technology. This process begins in the following chapter where we explore the diverse pathways disabled workers took to working with new technology.

 **7**

Pathways to work with new technology

This chapter begins the process of exploring in depth the employment experiences for disabled people working with new technology. From this point all research findings are those gleaned from the semi-structured interviews undertaken with a sub-sample of 30 disabled people, about the varied pathways they have taken en route to working with new technology. This will allow insights into the routes other disabled workers may need to follow if they are to gain access to such work. It also provides details of the extent to which entry into new technology work was planned or fortuitous. This has major implications for any policy points that emanate from this study. What is clear from the following is that there have been many routes to technology-inclusive work, many of which were shaped by the cultural and technical changes that have shaped employment more generally over the past 30 years. The experiences are varied and to a large extent unique; however, similarities can be extracted from the experiences to allow for six identifiable pathways to new technology work. These routes are ideal typifications which capture the essential qualities of participants' pathways to work with new technology (number out of 30 in brackets):

- *by choice* path – workers choosing to enter computing from their previous work (9);
- *rehabilitation* path – workers moving into new technology work after rehabilitation, assessment or retraining (4);
- *work change* path – workers who have begun to use new technology in their established job because of the developments in office practice (10);
- *early user* path – workers who went straight into new technology work (2);
- *forced* path – workers who were forced to enter new technology work or face redundancy and unemployment (2);
- *underemployed* – those who have obtained some work with new technology, but have never been able to use their full abilities. This group is still trying

to gain new technology employment of a more substantial kind, and the path is incomplete (3).

(In the following interview transcripts, bracketed details describe the participant's name (anonymized), employment status, impairment/s, whether they use mobility aids, and the barriers they faced in their employment at the time of interview. For unemployed participants, details are provided of their last employment.)

The by choice pathway to new technology

This was the second most common route into work with new technology. In this context 'choice' relates to those people who had chosen such work from a position of strength, that of already having skilled work. In most instances the employment was of a technical or scientific nature. This work, reported exclusively by men, would have brought workers into contact with analytical or computing equipment at some time before their own work was based on microchip technology. How then can these experiences be typified?

The following interviews provide evidence of the role of choice in some disabled people's entry to new-technology-inclusive work. The first comes from Ray, a former analytical chemist. In his work Ray was able to experiment with new technology:

> After that I moved to water chemistry. I didn't like this and over the years I got involved in the early forms of computing, computer graphics, they [employers] were desperate for people who could add one and one together. My boss, an analytical chemist, did the hard sums while I put them into computer form.
> (Ray, computer accounts manager, rheumatoid arthritis; environmental and technical barriers)

In Ray's instance, he had already entered computing proper before his arthritis had set in. The status and autonomy of his work in chemical analysis allowed him to move into computing. This was at a time when computing itself was in its infancy (early 1960s). The informal nature of computing at this time allowed him access without any formal qualifications. By the time his arthritis had become established, Ray admits to being senior enough to be able to shape the use he made of the technology he used. Ray's experience, although in some ways unique, is comparable to a number of other workers who had been able to choose to enter new technology work. John's experiences are in many ways a carbon copy of Ray's, except that the decision to shift into new technology work was prompted by impairment itself:

> While I was a chief experimental officer [chemicals] I was diagnosed as having multiple sclerosis. At the time I was doing chemical analysis, and that became too much as analysis was quite a physical process. When I was in the laboratories I was learning spreadsheets, I eventually real-

ized that this work would be better suited to my health circumstances. So I made a decision to request retraining. At the time I wasn't certain of the options with computerized chemical analysis, but I found that the shift was quite straightforward as colleagues in other departments of Axxon were already doing useful work with computer-based profiling of harmful substances.

(John, chief experimental officer, multiple sclerosis; environmental barriers)

John was able to move into database work, compiling listings of hazardous chemicals under the COSSH regulations. This work draws on his analytical skills, while allowing him to work in a more user-friendly environment:

My job now consists of opening the electronic mail, seeing what mes- sages you've got; and then I have to enter chemicals into a database. I do less of the actual physical analysis of chemicals, although that option still exists. My employers are quite flexible about my job content as long as we negotiate any changes.

(John)

Some of the by choice group left their previous employment because of a dislike of their work, and because they felt new technology work might pre- sent a new challenge to them. A number of these decisions were based on questions of employment preferences rather than consideration of changing physical status. Peter provides a good example of this. He was working for a government department, in one of its Scottish offices and was using desktop technology, but only in a very marginal way. However, he had a taste of working with new technology during his graduate studies in geology. He pro- fessed to not liking the work in West Kilcoyne and decided to move within the Civil Service to computing work. Peter's ability to make this internal shift was made easier because of his employment status as a graduate entry executive officer:

Obviously my scientific background helped and I knew people who were in computing, or who used computers. I had had a little experi- ence. Actually I did toy with a COBOL [programming language] course at university. I felt that I had a flair for computers and that they were a safe bet in terms of future work.

(Peter, data communications specialist, myalgic encephalomyelitis; environmental barriers)

The workers in the by choice group all shared an ability to move into new technology work from other high status work. Not all, however, had done hands-on work with computers before moving to new technology work, but most had by that time seen the possibilities of working with new technology. Two of this group remained in their previous employment but chose to base their work on new technology.

The two important characteristics of this group are that they are all senior workers, either by qualification or lengthy experience. They are all male and reflect the historic power of skilled male workers in having relative advantages in shaping their employment domain and the technology used in their work. The experiences of a number of this group can be seen as historically contingent, based as they are on being in the right place at an opportune moment. It is likely that the same voluntary shift into computing from other skilled work (without formal qualifications) will diminish as more people enter computing and skilled technology-based work (such as medical and chemical science work) via a qualificatory route. This has implications for any planned policies on new technology and disabled people.

The rehabilitation pathway

This second pathway into new technology work shares in common with the by choice grouping a voluntaristic entry into technology-inclusive work. However, this group is different, not simply because it was a less common pathway to new technology work, but also because the choice was made after a period of reorientation in the form of rehabilitation, assessment or retraining. However, only one of the disabled workers who had received rehabilitation felt that work with new technology had been facilitated in any way by this process. The identification and search for this work was the result of disabled people's own efforts, and it was clear that gaining work with new technology was in spite of the rehabilitation process, not because of it.

Gill provides a useful example of someone who entered new technology work after a number of years out of work, and who completed a number of taster courses on various topics. Having experienced what she sees as the ineptitude of rehabilitation workers, Gill identified new technology work as appropriate for her as a disabled person. The following comments relate to a period when Gill had given up hope of getting positive assistance from her disablement resettlement officer and had begun some home-based sewing work to try to make ends meet. She had already experienced a taster course in basic computer skills:

> It was during this time that I started working on keyboard skills. I wasn't too sure of the objective at that point, but sooner or later I knew I was going to need the skills to get a better job than sewing. I also bought a Spectrum computer at that time, it was an encouragement, I had found that I was able to do more than I thought, some of which came in handy in the job I took after that.
>
> (Gill, computer-based trainer, complex and multiple impairments, wheelchair user; attitude and environmental barriers)

Gill was able to move to a job she enjoyed after a number of false starts, which for her said more about the kinds of work available to a disabled woman than it did about her skills. For Gill the choice of new technology work was her own, based on the training she had received in the previous four years.

Gill's experience shares some features with that of Gordon; he also gained technology work after a period of rehabilitation. Here the term 'assessment' best sums up Gordon's situation. In Gordon's experience, a series of team-based professional assessments led to the conclusion that he had an aptitude for new technology work. As Gordon noted, 'This was something I was aware of, but I felt too threatened by the number of assessment staff involved in the decision, so I just kept quiet.' The process involved little in the way of hands-on work with hardware and software. Gordon also underwent a barrage of psychometric tests, writing, arithmetic and dexterity tests. As might be predicted from previous comments, the assessment process was not followed up with help to gain actual employment. Gordon again proved to be the main instigator of the process of finding his first job using new technology. On the advice given by the assessment team, Gordon notes:

> I was encouraged to go on to a national diploma, but the facilities at the college put me off, they were not fully accessible for me [as a wheelchair user]. Besides I wanted to go straight into employment. There was only one ramp in the building, and you had to go from one end of the building to the other to get to the car park.
>
> (Gordon, administration officer, spina bifida, wheelchair user; attitude and environmental barriers)

Although Gordon's employment was a mixed experience during the first few years, he puts this down to the supernumerary nature of much of it. One of these jobs was arranged by the now defunct Asset training company, which became the subject of a government investigation of its training standards.

Gordon has been able to enter technology-inclusive work with the indirect help of 'professional' assessment, but the final leverage came from a mixture of his own abilities with new technology and his own efforts to find suitable employment.

Ahmed also related his frustration at the lack of concrete support from rehabilitation and assessment staff, noting how they seemed to offer advice but not help. Ahmed received both medical and employment rehabilitation over a period of two years following spinal injury. The experience was mixed: while medical support was excellent, at no point had staff discussed Ahmed's previous employment in geological surveying or the possibility of using new technology to enhance his rehabilitation, as he noted:

> No effort was made on the employment front. I remember going to the occupational therapy department and playing dominoes. There was a PC less than a metre away from me, but nobody put it on, or even asked if I had any experience of them, or knew how they worked. This of course was one particular unit, the Podmoore Spinal Unit. Unfortunately it was the same at the Maudevale unit.
>
> (Ahmed, computer officer, spinal cord injury, wheelchair user; attitude and environmental barriers)

In this way the rehabilitation process began and ended with medical interventions. Ahmed was ill-prepared to enter the working world because the rehabilitation he received was of a very general kind, which he described as an attempt to build confidence, but without any sense of what that confidence might be used for.

As someone who had worked with computers before, and who had used complex seismological software applications, Ahmed eventually re-entered work with computers but at a very basic level as a computer officer. This in no way exploited his depth of computing skills; indeed the work does not fit into the computer worker category as his job was a form of data input and retrieval. However modest the work, Ahmed clearly identified work with PCs as important for a wheelchair user:

> I realized that since I couldn't do the geologist job anymore, I couldn't find myself restricted to manual work; so I identified computers as the right work. I had a background in using computers because I used them when I was originally a geologist working with seismic data and computer-based models of seismic activity and geological profiles.
>
> (Ahmed)

A useful comparison can be made between the by choice group and the rehabilitation pathways. Firstly, although in each instance choice was exercised at some point in the process of getting new technology work, in the case of the rehabilitation group, that choice was not made from a position of already having work. Secondly, this group's employment did not extend to what can be described as computer work, such as analysis or programming. This is a contrast to the by choice group, who were able to enter higher status computing work because of their already established employment status. It is possible to discern a difference in the histories of the computer worker and technology user groups, in that the pathway to new technology employment may be seen to be shaped by more than paper qualifications.

The work change path

This is the most common pathway to work with new technology. This path represents those disabled workers who have experienced technological changes in their office work, but whose job description remains broadly the same as before. The typical person here was a female worker (but two out of ten are men) who was previously a typist, secretary or clerical worker who now uses a word processor, visual display unit, e-mail and fax machines in their everyday work. Clearly in most instances the level of choice and the shaping of use of new technology was low, with employers usually introducing new technology unilaterally and for wider organizational or business motives. This does not mean that the experience of new technology was necessarily a negative one, but clearly any benefits observed and barriers reduced must be seen as fortuitous rather than planned. Here then are some typical comments about a worker's first encounters with new technology:

I have never been asked whether the technology my employer is introducing is suitable for me, not really. I am given the equipment, then just
choose where to put it. At the moment I am in my own office, but after
next month we are in a new open plan office; we have been told for
example, what technology will be introduced, but no choice was made
available as to the technology used.

(Val, senior personal secretary, polyarthritis; environmental
and attitude barriers)

Although not involved in the planning and adoption of new employment
technologies, Val noted that because she is a senior secretarial worker, she is
able to limit the amount of word processing and documents she produces
each day. She also stated that she had a high degree of autonomy in her work
and can choose when to walk about, and can delegate work of this kind. She
felt that junior staff with impairments would not have this flexibility, and
would have less chance to shape the way technology is used.

Joan offers an example of someone who has not been able to call the tune
over new technology use. The result is that Joan faces greater barriers in her
workplace not simply because of her impairment, but also due to her lack of
seniority. In the following, Joan describes the uncontrolled introduction of
new technology into her work as a secretary in a high street bank:

Actually, when we first got the computer system you couldn't get to it;
too many people wanted to use the system. That's why I started to work
at eight in the morning so that I could get things done, you see all that
pressure, you've got to get there to do all the work. In fact the typists got
to use them [PCs] before the secretaries. We were all a little bit wary of
it, but they said we had to use it.

(Joan, part-time secretary, multiple sclerosis; attitude,
environmental and technical barriers)

This process of introducing new technology without reference to the personal preferences of an employee was not always a negative experience.
Such a unilateral introduction was often fortuitously positive, as in the
experience of Denise. Denise first experienced new technology after a
number of years in office supervision following a stroke when she was 21.
She was working for a book distribution company when new technology was
introduced, and wider organizational changes occurred. She notes in a positive vein:

I was introduced to it while I was there [The Readers Club]. Before the
PC, we had to do letters by hand, you had to go to the typists then.
When the system was introduced many things went on to the computer. You could get the client's name and account details up on the
screen, alter a book order, cancel it, credit it. An excellent service. I
found that I had more control over my work and could keep myself in
the picture more readily. As someone with limited stamina, this was a
great boon to me. I could channel my energies more creatively. I still

had to move around to supervise, but I didn't have to move around to glean information as I had to before.

(Denise, purchasing officer, hemiplegia; attitude and environmental barriers)

When asked to compare her former manually based work with computerized book ordering she notes:'I enjoy it [PC-based work], I suppose I like to be the same as everybody else. So that I'm not unduly reliant on anyone else'.

The path to new technology work is further complicated by those workers using both mainstream technologies provided by their employer, and specialized technologies provided by the Employment Service's DAS workers. Here the path to new technology work may be less clear, even where the worker has always done essentially the same job. Mandy is a good example of this. As a blind secretary with many years' experience, Mandy had applied for and received an 'Optacon', a device which translates ordinary text into tactile figures. This was provided by the DAS in 1984, well before her employer had introduced mainstream technology to any significant degree. Mandy found that her secretarial work was significantly enhanced by the enabling potential of the technological devices provided. However, Mandy's pathway to these technological aids was to prove a tortuous and disabling one. She applied during the late 1980s for an updated package of mainstream PC and specialized speech equipment to allow her the full range of PC functions plus text output using a speech system. Mandy found that she was trapped between an intransigent employer and DAS officials, neither of whom were prepared to provide the mainstream technology, each seeing the other as the rightful provider of this non-specialist technology.

Mandy's path, then, proved to be a difficult one, one which was impeded by employer attitudes and bureaucratic rigidities. However, what Mandy still has in common with this broad work change group is that eventually her work changed technologically while her overall job description remained the same. The complicating factor in this example is that those changes were instigated by Mandy herself, and were slower to materialize than if her employer had instigated them.

The early user path

One pathway so far unmentioned is that of entering technology-inclusive work as a first job. There is no evidence here that this pathway was always the result of careful career planning, a move designed to seek out enabling working environments. However, given the increasing presence of new technology in the education and training of disabled people, this route is likely to become a commonly planned pathway for disabled people in the future. What then was the nature of this route to new technology work for the small number (2) who took it?

A distinction needs to be made between the two people to enter directly and stay in technology-based work. Although they are both graduates with a wide range of computing ability, one is a computer programmer while the other is a computer-based university lecturer. In the case of the programmer, entry into programming was a direct choice after leaving university. Although not viewed in terms of enabling technology, Stewart saw new technology work as an arena in which he could express his abilities as a person with a hearing impairment more than in most other work. In this sense this is the sum total of his pathway to IT work, with no other experiences intervening to shape his decision to enter.

It is worth noting that regardless of Stewart's ease of entry into programming, and his perception of it being a more positive environment for a person with a hearing impairment, he was to be proven wrong. His direct entry into computer work is looked back on with regret. Here are his accounts of his unceremonious and rushed induction into programming, one which took little account of his preferences:

> I entered as a direct entrant to executive officer and I did an introductory training course in programming, which was shorter than it should have been. I have to say that with hindsight I think I was discriminated against – six weeks after I started at the Civil Service the training course was cut short. I had missed the preliminary induction course which would normally make you feel assimilated. I was the only disabled person on the course. No real support was given for my needs. It was assumed that I could hear enough of what the trainer said. Really I needed extra time to absorb the fundamental building blocks of the programming training.
>   (Stewart, programmer, hearing impairment; attitude,
>   environmental and technical barriers)

The very different experience of the other worker to enter his first job with new technology suggests that there is nothing inherently problematic about this path. Alex, a university lecturer, entered his career with the aim of combining an academic career with a suitable environment for a disabled person. Although his limitations were slight compared to today, through time, he has decided to use new technology to an increasing extent in order to bring his working environment to him, rather than the other way around. As with Stewart, by directly entering technology-based work he did not have any other employment experiences with which to compare himself. What then were his early employment experiences?

Alex began as a research officer using computers to run large datasets for quantitative research. Although computer-based, this sort of work was actually very tiring, with plenty of leg work shifting piles of paper from one building to another. Alex vowed that regardless of the computer support, he would not do number-crunching mainframe work again, but he realized the overall value of computers for him at this early stage. His changing academic work and the development of desktop personal computers allowed him to use technology in a way that reduced the non-disabled demands of the university environment. Although he did not want to stay in mainframe work, he admits his indebtedness to this work in giving him hands-on experience and an interest in computing. An element of fortuitousness also pervades Alex's early experience of technology, as the following story expresses:

The first time that I used technology would be the summer of 1967 in a summer job. I worked for the Paper Corporation in the United States, which is a trade association. I was involved in making statistical forecasts; it was an electronically sophisticated office with computer terminals through to large mainframes.

(Alex, senior lecturer, syringomyelia, spinal muscular atrophy and myeloma, wheelchair user; environmental barriers)

What is clear from these experiences of directly entering technology-inclusive work is that within the same route, very different experiences resulted. In Alex's case, although the first job was not ideal, the experience was invaluable and later led to new technology work in a supportive university environment. This contrasts diametrically with Stewart's experience of an unsupported working life, which takes little account of his stated needs.

Clearly, the only common features of these two experiences are the direct entry into technology-inclusive work, and the realization of the potential new technology can have in the working lives of disabled people. Apart from these two main similarities the experiences could not be more different. This contrast illustrates that pathways to new technology can tell us little about the likely experiences people might have when they finally get to technology-inclusive work. It also supports the notion of new technology only having benefits for disabled workers when it accompanies positive attitudes and an enabling working environment more generally. A complete contrast to this route is offered in the following assessment of the two people whose pathway to IT work was via a forced route.

The forced pathway

Two disabled participants described their path to new technology in terms of being forced to enter work with new technology. William's experience was that if he refused to accept a shift to new technology work, he would have been made redundant. Trevor had been faced with a similar ultimatum when applying for research work in the Civil Service and was told that he would only be considered for programming work.

William's experience was that he had wanted to go into medicine, but because his schooling and education did not prepare him for this, he took the option of laboratory work in a private sector medical research company. Unfortunately his work was not designed to include people with impairments. This was exacerbated by William's own uncertainty about his suitability for the exact tasks he was given. This mismatch between physical status and task meant that he was often introduced to grossly inappropriate work in a hostile environment. The result was a string of minor disasters which put his and other workers' health at risk. After much relocation into equally unsuitable work, the decision was made to place William in a desk job, something that was against his own preference to do an appropriately designed job in the laboratory context. William explains this whole process very graphically:

I entered computer programming after a chain of accidents and incidents. When I started at the research company in 1970 I was allowed in because I was very enthusiastic, and I could get a green card. I started in the pathology lab, but had an accident clearing up. I spilt something that damaged my lung and throat. They tried to get rid of me but I refused, so they had to relocate me. So I moved into microbiology. But they began to develop a product that was harmful related to the test material for thalidomide. This only grows on mutagenic material. As I have to get close to my work, and as the material could kill me if it were ingested, I was taken out of there.

(William, unemployed programmer, visual impairment; attitude, environmental and technical barriers)

Having experienced a number of problems in the inadequately supported environment of the laboratory, the decision was made to move William out of chemical work. From the employer's point of view this forced move was justified as it was due to William's 'unsuitability' for such work. However, a barriers approach would view this process the other way: visual aids, job redesign and colleague support could have been made available on terms suitable to both William and his employers. However, these steps were not taken, and William continued to be shunted about with little attention to his own preferences. What is fortunate about William's later experiences was that the trial and error of this shunting process was eventually going to end in him finding work which he suggests exploited his abilities. After another period of relocation into warehouse work, where even more unsuitable work led to a pallet of metal falling on him, William was finally moved to desk work. He takes up the story:

After the accident they said: 'Right, let's get him a desk job.' So they sent me over to the computer department, saying: 'Here is a bloke with a brain in his head – keep him away from everything, but use him.' We mutually disagreed about this relocation but after a fortnight I agreed to take it, because I was told there was no alternative.

(William)

Although William's work developed rapidly with his entry into programming, he reported a severe lack of support. However, the fortuitous suitability of programming was clear as a controllable technology. Although it was rather a bumpy road to new technology work, the forcing of William to do alternative work or leave was in this instance the antecedent to valuable work with computers. Sadly, William was made redundant in 1987, 13 years after this unpropitious start in computing. He has not been able to find work since.

Trevor applied for an appointment in the Civil Service researching crime because he felt it would make full use of his MA in criminology. He was prepared to relocate from his native north-east of England to get work in criminological research for the Home Office. Trevor was accepted for interview, but his success in that interview was shattered when he was informed that he would be most welcome in the Civil Service, but that he would have to enter programming work as a direct entry executive officer. So unlike William's experience of being forced into computing work or face losing his job, Trevor was effectively forced into his first full-time permanent post. The memory of this unceremonious entry to programming is still a vivid one for Trevor:

> I applied to the Civil Service in 1985; I was exempt from their executive officer exams because of sight limitations. There were a lot of pictorial associations in the tests. They said they were interested in interviewing me because of my qualifications. They took me down to Whitehall for a series of tests, then I was taken to their centre for blind programmer trainees. I had an aptitude test there. It was very much geared for the visually handicapped. I then had an interview I enjoyed. There was a blind person on the panel. I stated that I wanted to do Home Office-related work, and did not want to be a programmer. I felt that they were pushing me to this. The blind person said that I would have to do programming if I was to become a civil servant, because that's the best course for the likes of us. They concluded that they couldn't afford to put a blind person into a traditional post.
>
> (Trevor, programmer, visual impairment; attitude, environmental
> and technical barriers)

Trevor finally accepted that he had no choice and that he would have to enter programming. As with William's experience of computer work, he later found that he enjoyed the work, and given that he received much more technical support than William, was able to use his abilities quite extensively. The ambivalence expressed by both Trevor and William about their first perceptions of computing soon faded away as they realized the suitability of the work for an employee with a visual impairment. However, it is worth remembering the fortuitous – that is, unplanned – nature of these benefits. These examples of forced pathways to computing work, would arguably not occur if assessment for employability was reframed to test aptitudes and skills in diverse ways. The initial perception of work-based technology use would also be less problematic if there was more computer literacy among disabled people and if their exercise of choice was more in evidence.

The underemployed: the impeded pathway to IT work

This small group (3) is made up of those workers who, although reporting significant experience and skill development in their work with new technology, feel that their abilities have been grossly underemployed. Each worker expressed a sense of frustration that meaningful work had eluded them. Their experiences can be summed up as a series of false dawns, endless training schemes, employment initiatives and supernumerary work. Here, the pathway to technology work was one littered with barriers created by employers and not erased by Employment Service staff. The experiences of Clive and Brian are representative of this group. Clive's experience was of an early belief that his abilities with new technology would eventually lead to employment, and that this work would be largely on his own terms, that is, about 25 hours per week.

Clive had completed a Royal Society of Arts course in spreadsheets, word processing and database work. Despite having had 15 years' experience of part-time sheltered employment doing database and spreadsheet work, Clive has still not managed to secure work with new technology on his own terms. When asked why the pathway to new technology work has been so halting, he points to the low expectations of trainers and employers in failing to develop and recognize his abilities. Clive explains why, after so much experience, he has chosen to go self-employed (2–3 hours per month):

I couldn't find suitable work outside, at first the part-time [sheltered] work was more like occupational therapy. I wanted to be independent, as I'm a very independent person. Lately I have gone it alone and started doing a consultancy-based job. I am still doing similar hours, but under my own steam. I organize my time and work, and I *don't* get supervised by the CP Society.

(Clive, computer consultant, cerebral palsy, wheelchair user; attitude and environmental barriers)

He goes on to describe his reasons for wanting more substantial employment:

I want to be able to say I can do this, and to be able to hold my head up high, and not be ashamed of being unemployed. At present I feel very frustrated, a prisoner of my own brain.

(Clive)

This sense of frustrated ability, the impeded pathway to fulfilling employment, is less potent in Brian's experiences, but his frustration is still very much in evidence. Brian has also done many years of work with computers, especially in programming. Many of these programming skills were gained at the Royal Training College, where he completed an introductory course. Brian has had a number of years' experience in a sheltered training environment where he has helped establish a cooperative, producing specialist software designed to aid other disabled people in computer-assisted learning. However, Brian's activities in the cooperative are declining as its success has been in some doubt.

Brian feels that his wider technological and design abilities have never been fully used, and that as a mature man with multiple sclerosis he is unlikely to achieve work equal to his abilities. Brian explains how he got his first real experience of using his new technology skills:

Someone from the [then] Leathmill professional workshop approached me, saying 'We want some people to work with us, how do you feel about that?' When I went there it was on a more-or-less voluntary basis. But I enjoyed the experience as we moved from nought to programming in the time that I was there. I ended up co-writing educational software designed for kids with mental handicaps. Our aim was to make this a commercially successful venture, but one that helped other disabled people benefit from computers. The profits were secondary really.

> (Brian, voluntary co-director, multiple sclerosis, wheelchair user;
> attitude and environmental barriers)

All of Brian's work has since been on a voluntary or nominally waged basis. He feels that his full range of abilities has been left dormant, save for his own work on computers which he does for his own self-respect. Brian, as with Clive, feels that he has been led into a sense of false security by the sheltered programmes he has been involved with. While it is likely that they would not have developed as many skills as they have without the sheltered work, their path may well have been stymied by the sheltered experience. As Brian notes about his frustrated abilities with technology:

I do some work for the [sheltered] CP Society resource centre and my course work for my computing certificate at Leek University, but I am waiting for action really. I am an expert at the waiting game. I am so aware of what I can do, other people rarely get to see just what I can do with computers.

> (Brian)

Conclusion

The interviews in this chapter represent the mixture of pathways disabled people have followed on the road to new technology work. The range of experiences suggests that the directness and enabling/disabling qualities of these paths are not easy to predict. However, they provide optimism about the plurality of means by which other disabled people might enter such work. A reading of the variety of pathways and experiences suggests that there was no golden road to the enabling use of new technology, and that both good and bad experiences were evident in all routes.

A number of preliminary points came out of the findings as a whole. Firstly, that the route to enabling technology use was easier to manipulate if the person was already in high status employment. Such a high employment status allowed for more shaping of how, when and under what circumstances new technology was used.

Secondly, female workers were more likely to experience imposed technological change. Here the greater concentration of women in lower status office work suggests that they may be more exposed to the broader dynamics that shape organizations' use of new technology. This need not be a bad experience, but it is clear that women were overrepresented in the work change category, and this may suggest that they have less scope to shape the way technology is introduced and used. Conversely, women were less likely to be found in computing work, while those in such high status computer work seemed at first sight to have had more control of technological change.

Having looked at diverse pathways to using new technology, the next chapter examines the reported benefits of new technology and how they can ameliorate (to some extent) workplace barriers. It also looks at how, in some instances, new technology has altered an individual's perception of the disability problem.

 **8**

Enabling technology: the benefits of new technology

This chapter explores the benefits of new technology in the working lives of the disabled people researched. As this work is premised on a barriers model, the focus will be on the way new technology has enabled workers to overcome or reduce workplace barriers. However, this chapter focuses primarily on environmental barriers because the greatest degree of reported benefits cluster around their reduction, and because attitude and technical barriers seemed to have been most resistant to change. I do not mean to suggest that attitudes have not changed at all; evidence of widespread attitude barriers, however, is reflected in their prominent position in the next chapter on remaining barriers to enabling employment. In examining the extent and nature of benefits for disabled workers, it is important to bear in mind the broad comparative categories established earlier. For example, attention will be given to any differences in benefits between computer workers and technology users, and also between those using mainstream and specialized technologies.

Bringing down the shameful walls of exclusion

The capacity of new technology to reduce or eliminate environmental barriers was the benefit most commonly cited by participants. Environmental barriers were defined as any physical structure, work practice or technology which was seen to have limited people with impairments in the employment environment. At its most general, new technology provided more choice and ease of getting things done. Other benefits included more focused working environments (where a multiplicity of tasks are concentrated into one workstation), a more equalized workplace, and enhanced levels of communication and participation for some disabled people.

What then were the detailed benefits of new technology in reducing environmental barriers? There was an overall reduction in mobility requirements. Here, new technology had allowed a redefinition of the disabled person's working environment – more specifically, the 'core text' of the employment domain had been brought closer to the disabled worker. Enhanced access to work was expressed in terms of better access to filing, sending messages, document retrieval, paper and text handling. Paul, a spinal-injured systems engineer, provides a general image of new technology benefits:

> The main benefit for me is that I am able to do a multiplicity of tasks in one place. This is made even easier by 'Windows', as it has a clock and a calculator. I suppose I feel more in control of my work, and feel confident that I can get access to what my colleagues are doing without having to walk about.
>
> (Paul, systems engineer, spinal-injured, uses crutches; environmental barriers)

Another comment, this time from Gill, a computer-based trainer, refers to the physical ease of computer use:

> Computing can be done without standing. I can sit next to the trainee, given that a lot of work is one-to-one; also I don't have to cart stuff around, all the information can be stored on the computer. I can work for much longer with computer-based training, and concentrate on the training bit. I used to spend a lot of time standing in front of the trainees; although it was more communal, it was very tiring. My joints would soon become painful. With IT it is OK to sit down to work. PCs require the kind of activities that I can do best. I still get tired quickly, but it's a major improvement.
>
> (Gill, computer-based trainer, complex and multiple impairments following an accident, wheelchair user; attitude and environmental barriers)

The scarcity of energy associated with some impairments and the ability to channel this energy was also noted by Jane. Jane, a purchasing officer with polio, has faced significant environmental barriers in her workplace due to a reliance on manual text production, inappropriate technology and bulky filing methods used in her purchasing department. The advent of new technology use has gone some way to reducing these demands:

> The PC is less tiring than the electronic typewriter, because with that you are reaching for the paper tray, going for files and having to put them back. As you can imagine, the purchasing files held all of the purchase orders we processed. I suppose the bigger files could be as heavy as a [2.5 kg] bag of potatoes. For me that has proved very difficult. The partial move to computers makes my work much easier. I've realized that by using new technology I can do my job much better. I only wish that it had been introduced before. Actually, when I think about it, the

old manual system could have been redesigned long ago so that the files were smaller and more manageable. But I never had a lot of say in how we worked. As a disabled woman I felt that I was vulnerable, and didn't want to rock the boat.

(Jane, purchasing officer, polio, uses sticks;
attitude and environmental barriers)

In some instances where disabled people worked more substantially with new technology, as with many of the computer worker group, new technology was consciously used to reduce the need to travel unnecessary distances. Ray, a middle manager with rheumatoid arthritis, is quite typical of this group:

I use the keyboard for virtually all communications and tasks, everything apart from signing my name. Over time I became acutely aware of just what the computer allows me to do. I think anyone with RA is conscious of how they use their energy. I'm no exception. I use every available labour-saving device on the machine. As a bit of a 'techno' I think I know how to get the best out of the software. I can manage my staff without the need to traipse around the office complex. Bear in mind the environment here is a hotchpotch of buildings. Some are very accessible, others are a nightmare. I've now got the choice. Sometimes I really feel the need to walk, other times I will use the e-mail and phone to do my work. I'm only really doing what most workers do, but as someone with RA I'm more conscious of this.

(Ray, computer accounts manager, rheumatoid arthritis;
environmental and technical barriers)

Similarly, Dennis's comments encapsulate the benefits of reduced mobility barriers:

With the old manual systems the work was more tedious, your work had to be spread out, with a lot of paper to use. With the PC, it's all on one screen. For a disabled person you haven't got to lump walloping great files around.

(Dennis, self-employed accountant, polio, wheelchair user;
environmental barriers)

Similarly Gill notes how she consciously exploits the focused nature of PC working:

I probably keep things on the database longer than most others would. If I file something on my own PC, it means that I'm less likely to lose it than a paper copy. I also try to put all of my admin on one computer. This way I reduce my energy output and I can keep tabs on most aspects of my work in just one place. I do anything to avoid walking, as I soon get pains if I walk too far. I have developed a way of bringing most of my work to me. None of my colleagues mind, they seem happy for me to work that way. It usually means, implicitly, that if I need to meet a colleague, they come to me rather than the other way about. Additionally, I will sit making notes on to the PC as someone speaks to me. This might seem a bit odd, but it's my way of economizing on physical activity. It means I don't have to run around as much, checking what I've said in these meetings.

> (Gill, computer-based trainer, complex and multiple impairments
> following an accident, wheelchair user; attitude and
> environmental barriers)

Gill's comments express a common theme in the study: how new technology can help people work in a flexible way. John, a chief experimental officer in a private laboratory, notes:

> The technology gives me the option to work in a particular way. When I'm fit I tend to do a mix of computer-based and general admin work, opening mail, helping with analysis. When my MS is active I tend to stick to the work on the COSSH register. This I do on the PC. The work is less tiring and I work at my own pace on the register. I suppose I'm lucky in having a key facet of my work on the PC working on my own. This way I'm not paced by colleagues. But I can choose to work with them when the MS abates. The technology and my employer's favourable attitudes together make for a flexible arrangement.

> (John, chief experimental officer, multiple sclerosis;
> attitude and environmental barriers)

Comments were sometimes more explicit about a particular form of new technology that had reduced physical barriers. Alan, a library worker with multiple sclerosis, noted that:

> A number of databases are on CD-ROM, many were huge tomes, citation indexes and so on; this work could involve a lot of cross-referencing. With the CD-ROM you can do work more easily, it is less physical, less fiddly. Much of the time now I catalogue sitting down at the computer terminal. The CDs are all in the one place, rather than being volumes on the shelf. Before I would have to go to each part of the library for the different databases.

> (Alan, senior library assistant, multiple sclerosis, uses a walking
> frame; attitude and environmental barriers)

Val, a personal secretary with rheumatoid arthritis, makes an equally specific reference, this time to the value of fax machines:

> Using the fax stops me having to go to the [mail] dispatch point, it saves me writing too as I can send the same document a number of times. I certainly make it work for me. Also the new high quality fax paper means less unnecessary trips to the photocopier; previously shiny paper was of an inferior standard and was copied before managers received it.

> (Val, senior secretary, rheumatoid arthritis;
> attitude and environmental barriers)

From this initial examination, the benefits of using new technology in reducing workplace barriers were clearly evident across a range of employment, impairments and severity of impairments. The reduction of physical barriers and the facilitation of abilities were reported as mundane everyday benefits. This supports a key assertion made at the early stages of this research: the promise of technology relates as much to its widespread availability as it does to the power of dramatic 'state-of-the-art' interventions.

Competing on more equal terms

A number of people said that they had benefited from the way new technology had redefined their work and allowed their abilities to surface. Here the changing environment produced by new technology was seen as particularly beneficial for disabled workers. As all of the examples given are for mainstream technology, the benefits are not unique to the workers with impairments; the participants thought there was added significance for disabled workers because new technology provided a more equal working environment. A good example is provided by Joan, a secretary with multiple sclerosis:

> The word processor is useful when you have to type standard letters over and over again – all you need to do on the word processor is to put the names and addresses in. This leaves me with more energy to do other things. It's mainly the lighter keyboard and being able to have everything on the screen. To cut and paste, not having to type the whole thing again. I work with three other secretaries and can say categorically that I can do as much work as my colleagues using a word processor. I don't think I could have said the same about manual typing.
>
> (Joan, secretary, multiple sclerosis; attitude,
> environmental and technical barriers)

For Joan, new technology does not make the difference between working and not working – she admits that she could work with older equipment – but it has allowed her to conserve energy on unnecessary tasks: consequently she is able to compete on more equal terms with non-disabled workers. This theme of equalization was a fairly common remark from both technology users and computer workers alike. Here, Barry, a self-employed computer consultant, explains this feeling of enhanced personal status:

> There's no doubt about it in my mind that technology of the sort that I'm using here, PCs, etc., do enable me to work very much on an equal footing as an able-bodied person. What I find is that you survive the physical demands of the workplace much more. Although I'm self-employed, I do a lot of project work with old contacts. I feel that in this [work] I'm as capable as anyone else. I can compare this with the manual wiring work I used to do. I never felt on a par with colleagues;

that kind of work was survival of the fittest. I can do more than survive with new technology. I suppose it sounds arrogant, but I'm probably better than many in this area. I've found a kind of niche where I'm able to flourish. Although the work is erratic, I think computing has allowed me some degree of equality in employment terms.

(Barry, self-employed computer consultant, polio; environmental barriers)

Ahmed, a computer officer, makes a similar point about employment equality. He discusses equality in terms of the standard of work produced, and equality of appearances, Ahmed explains:

When I'm behind the PC I feel like anybody else, there is no restriction. Other people have to sit down to be proficient. So we become equal. Also, it is much easier for me to write a letter [with a PC] as my writing is deteriorating. So desktop work puts me on the same level as others . . . in more ways than one.

(Ahmed, computer officer, spinal cord injury, wheelchair user; attitude and environmental barriers)

The most significant single feature of the preceding interviews seems to be that mainstream new technology, if used in an enabling way, allows work to be done in a way that provides greater expression of abilities, and in some instances provides greater equality between disabled and non-disabled people. Unfortunately, 'greater equality' is the appropriate term to use here, which does not mean full equality. The suggestion that work with new technology had facilitated full equality was rejected.

Bringing it all back home: the benefits of homeworking with new technology

The potential for new technology in facilitating access to employment and to flexible working arrangements is epitomized in the responses from the three disabled homeworkers taking part in this study. Here, the notion of bringing the 'core text' of work to disabled workers is clearly a beneficial one, as Dennis, a disabled self-employed accountant, notes:

IT has made homeworking more realistic. The barrier of getting to work and coping with the working environment is particularly bad especially in winter. I am a slow starter in the morning so that time at which the rush hour finishes is the time at which you're ready to work [at home]. Now with this system [a PC] a disabled person is not different to any other user. Disability [impairment] is irrelevant. I think technology has challenged the whole idea of having to get to work being a physical exercise. I still have health problems related to polio but I'm far more effective at my work when I'm working from home. Being self-employed has aided this effectiveness, as I'm free to work at times that suit me best. If I want to rest mid-afternoon I can. I will then work into the evening. New technology is essentially 'round the clock': answerphones, modems, faxes, e-mail. The possibilities are endless, all we lack is imaginative employers.

(Dennis, self-employed and home-based accountant, wheelchair user, polio; environmental barriers)

Peter, a telematics specialist with ME, also noted the benefits of home-working as a flexible form of employment:

The greatest benefit is the equipment being at home; this increases the flexibility of my working hours. The benefit to my employers is that you do not have to forfeit skilled key staff, even though they have a limiting condition. I have very flexible employers, who know that I can be left to get on with my work. I still go into work a couple of times a week for team meetings, the rest is done by telephone.

(Peter, data communications specialist, myalgic encephalomyelitis; environmental barriers)

Another benefit cited by disabled homeworkers was both the reduction in stress levels and the freedom from the extraneous interferences that characterize modern office settings, particularly open-plan offices. As Peter notes:

I enjoy the peace and quiet of working at home. I don't really like the hubbub of the general office. You get less interruptions and you don't have to keep getting up to answer other people's phones. I'm sure you can do things five times faster at home. Fifteen hours at home might be the equivalent of a full week in an office for me. By the time I've got there, fought my way through the office screens and logged on, I'm already feeling tired. I have a separate room here [at home] where I work. This way I keep my work and leisure separate. I don't think I'd like to be working and relaxing in the same space. But I have my own controlled space which is neither the office nor 'home' as such, but a room that I see as somewhere in-between. I think the words 'homework' put some people off as they think home is sacred, that it is significant because it's not associated with work. I think we need a new term to describe this sort of working from home. I didn't have any real choice but to work at home given the ME, but this way of working is ideal. I am not that gregarious anyway, this is fortuitous. I can see how some people would miss the hubbub of the office.

(Peter)

The desire to combine home and office work was borne out in Alex's comments:

For me to do my job optimally, the workplace has to be more than a single place. I like to have the choice over where I work on a given day. Some days I feel that I need to work from home as the journey to the university and the added physical demands of a large complex would prove difficult. However, team meetings, course preparation and library use all mean that I need to go to the university, to my office. I wouldn't like to be at home for an indefinite period, it can be quite isolating. I have the choice to work in both places and I exercise that choice. If my condition deteriorated I might find the journey too difficult and would try to use teleworking more extensively.

(Alex, university lecturer, syringomyelia, spinal muscular atrophy and myeloma, wheelchair user; environmental barriers)

The decision by employers to have employees working from home was not seen as an unalloyed benefit for all parties. Disabled homeworkers stressed that the decision should be driven by themselves, and that homeworking should not be used by employers to get round the need to change workplace barriers. This use of homeworking was seen as less likely where disabled people were allowed choice in the decision to homework. In some instances, disabled workers felt they might opt to work from home at the first opportunity; other comments suggested that homeworking would be a last resort, as Richard says:

The basing of work at home would be a last resort. I prefer to get out of the house and have the contacts with my colleagues. As I work in planning I have to work as a team. Electronically this is possible, but such electronic team working relies on a high degree of cooperation and coordination. Also I would lose touch with reality working at home for too long. There is something about the personal contact I experience at work. So, the option of homeworking is there, but I'll only do it if I absolutely have to. I would still insist on going into the office when I could manage it.

(Richard, senior planning officer, multiple sclerosis, wheelchair user; attitude and environmental barriers)

The subject is reiterated by Peter, who although admitting to enjoying being out of the sway of office activity generally, did concede that homeworking can be isolating:

I am a bit worried about the isolation of working at home. I would like to go into the office for a couple of mornings a week. I think you've also got to be very organized and self-disciplined to work at home.

(Peter, computer telecommunications specialist, myalgic encephalomyelitis; environmental barriers)

Although homeworking conditions were not ideal for two of the three homeworkers interviewed, the value of homework was unquestionable in all three instances:

New technology allows me to work at home, that's very important for my future, that's why I would like a modem [computer phone link]. I work at home at the moment, but I still have to go to the office once a month. So, I'm half way to an ideal situation. I don't think I could cope with a typical office. I've had bad experiences of being interviewed for jobs where I just know I'm not going to be able to get around because of the steps, toilets or what have you. I know that I can work at my best at home or in an adapted workshop. I don't think I could always manage a full working week, but being at home and as a software consultant I think I could easily make ends meet.

(Clive, self-employed computer consultant, cerebral palsy;
attitude and environmental barriers)

Dennis saw the combination of homeworking and self-employment as the best arrangement for someone with a physical impairment. Dennis worked for many years as a salaried accountant, although he found that it constrained his autonomy as a disabled person and as an accountant. He admits, however, that the experience gave him the contacts needed to start self-employment from home. Dennis keeps in contact with his clients and business associates via electronic means and by extensive use of telecommunications. Here, he discusses the configured benefits of self-employment from home:

I like being my own boss, and being a disabled person, it does give me the flexibility to pace myself. For an employee, you are either *in* or *out* of the office. Now this would be a major issue if I was off-colour, if I had a bad chest [polio-related]. That might stop me going to work completely. Now, at home, I would still put in a few hours where I could. I work odd hours by conventional standards, but it suits me. I am a successful accountant at the end of the day.

(Dennis, self-employed accountant, polio, wheelchair user;
environmental barriers)

Clearly, new information and communications technology together (collectively termed 'telematics') allow a substantial redefinition of the character of work. This is true of both self-employment and employment from home using new technologies. In the case of paid employment, homeworking can be seen to reverse some aspects of the capitalist labour process (Marx 1954: 477; Littler 1982) in relocating the focus and organizational minutiae of work into the domestic sphere. Here the impulse to separate home and work might be seen to have been reversed. Here too, in both self-employment and employment at home, the likelihood of reduced direct supervision is enhanced. This is particularly true of self-employment, where the severing of economic activity from the sale of labour power is established, providing the potential for even greater autonomy.

Although the development of telematics has made pacing, supervision and surveillance easier (Lyon 1988: 156), the use of new technology in homeworking settings is driven by a multiplicity of factors, and it would be wrong to assume that this presents an inherent danger for disabled homeworkers. While optimism about homeworking with new technology should not be overstated or overgeneralized (Hakim 1985; Allen and Wolkowitz 1987; Pennington and Westover 1989), it is worth reflecting that poor homeworking is often the result of a relocation of already low paid, labour-intensive work into the domestic sphere. This type of homeworking is often manual work, performed by women and often unregulated. It is also equally important to identify good homeworking arrangements where they exist. The above examples of disabled homeworking were not in all instances ideal.

The future potential of supported homeworking and self-employment with new technology cannot be overestimated, however. The issues arising are, firstly, that disabled people and employers need to be made more aware of the possibility of homeworking with new technology. Secondly, disabled employees should be given the choice to work at home, but not at the exclusion of direct contact with employers and colleagues. Homeworking can then offer highly flexible employment, spatially and temporally. Flexibility, however, should continue to include the possibility of combinations of home and office working where this is a disabled employee's own stated preference. These issues will be explored further in the policy recommendations made in the final chapter of this work.

Communicating ability: new technology and enhanced communication

Another key benefit reported in the research was the power of new technology to contribute to the reduction of communication barriers, defined as limits to the spoken and printed word. Here benefits attach to the opening up of textual communication. Also the use of specialized technologies reportedly reduced communication barriers.

Before exploring the disabled workers' own comments on communication benefits, it is worth restating the underlying principles. Much communication at work has been exclusionary and ignored the needs of people with sensory impairments. This has traditionally meant that those with sensory impairments have not had equal access to, and use of, communicative resources. What is important is that communicative involvement can be understood on two levels: firstly, that of the immediate communication process – for example, the communication of facts and data; secondly, and perhaps more importantly, that of the person communicating abilities and attributes. For our purposes, the two forms of historically denied communication can be labelled *immediate* and *expressive* communication. Together, benefits can operate where new technology is used in an enabling (if imperfect) way to enhance both immediate and expressive forms of communication.

Enabling immediate communication

The potential of new technologies to reduce communication barriers, and the scope for a plurality of communication options, is conveyed graphically in the following accounts. As mentioned above, the reduction of communication barriers and the enhanced options surrounding workplace communication benefited mainly (but not exclusively) workers with sensory impairments. Here both computer workers and technology users with sensory impairments provided evidence of the enabling potential of mainstream and specialized technologies. However, specialized technologies were cited more often as enabling enhanced communication.

Specialized technology ranged from a full battery of expensive translative technologies, changing text to speech output for example, through to ad hoc screen enlargement packages for workers with visual impairments. In order to disaggregate the communicative benefits cited by the disabled participants it was necessary to separate them into enhanced 'communication receipt' and enhanced 'communication production'. The former refers to choices in the way communications are received, while the latter is related to choices in the production of communications. The assessment of benefits will begin by looking at 'communication receipt'. Access to receiving messages in a beneficial form was clearly facilitated by the technology used by some workers. Tony, a computer services manager with a visual impairment, is representative of wider experiences:

> I can read the enlarged screen better than paper-based text, so it's making reading a lot easier, also it's the ability to alter the contrast on a PC, plus you can change the colours. Fairly simple basic things, but it makes a difference. The other big advantage is the spell checker. If you can't see very well you tend to miss incorrect spellings. This catches most of them. There is nothing worse than not having accurate information to hand. I read reports, minutes and memos quickly and easily with the enlarging software. I encourage colleagues to send me stuff on disc or e-mail so that I don't have to read too many documents with my hand lens.
>
> (Tony, computer services manager, visual impairment; environmental barriers)

Trevor makes similar comments about the large screen, but in his experience the specialized equipment not only made his communication easier but also made his programming work possible:

> I wouldn't be able to programme if it wasn't for the large screen and the speed of being able to do the job, and error reduction. I used to have clerical help when I was having to read the small print. But now I have slung a lot into the word processor and mainframe. I can access quite quickly with the [enlarged] screen, it's enhanced my independence. Written communication is the biggest most fundamental boost I've had, I can express myself, do better work.
>
> (Trevor, programmer, visual impairment; attitude, environment and technical barriers)

For workers with visual impairments faced with a working environment based predominantly on conventional text, the chance to access printed material via Optacon, scanners, jottas and speech output equipment, is an obvious boon. Mandy is an example of a blind worker only recently able to manipulate the receipt of text – evident in her still fresh praise for the speech output system she has acquired:

> There is no way I could access a computer with just a monitor.You would have to tell me which keys to press. Speech is the most marvellous miracle that's happened. I am glad that we [disabled people] are not being left behind. Speech output gives me access to things that other workers take for granted, access to documents, which are the essence of office work, whichever area you happen to be working in. I feel that I'm up with wider office changes and not left standing by the changes in technology.
>
> (Mandy, secretary, blind; attitude and environment barriers)

A similar level of enthusiasm was evident in the comments of Graham, a blind computer programmer, this time about e-mail, a mainstream facility but one which was still a relatively novel communication tool in 1992:

> E-mail has had special benefits for me as a blind person. With it I can get access to memos and details of what's going on in my section. I can communicate without having to walk about as well. So I don't have as much trudging to do. It is better than paper communication for me as it is not as easily mislaid and all of the messages are in the same place. For someone who is blind, this is an important focus for communication. I use a Brailler to get access to lengthy or urgent mail.
>
> (Graham, programmer, blind;
> attitude, environmental and technical barriers)

Graham singles out e-mail for its wider value in communication. In addition to e-mail, Graham uses an electronic scanner which scans conventional text into the personal computer. The examples of Mandy and Graham show how a package of sophisticated technologies can transform their immediate communication environment. While these are indispensable adjuncts to the enabling process, not all enabling tools cited were the result of planned specialized provision nor particularly sophisticated, as William's early experiences of programming suggest:

> IBM for some reason had a 'scalloped out' keyboard, and they put little dots on strategic points. Even though it was a standard keyboard, the dots meant that you could locate by running your fingers along the keyboard. I'm not sure whether this scalloping was designed for disabled people, or the dots on the keyboard. But they had the affect of helping people with dexterity and sight problems use the keyboard more easily.
>
> (William, unemployed programmer, visual impairment;
> attitude, environmental and technical barriers)

Other comments were made in this vein, suggesting that low technology, often unplanned features of new technology, both hard and software, have also been beneficial in the enabling process. Having looked at some typical

comments about communication receipt, what of communication production? This completes the cycle of immediate communication, and is as important a factor in the lives of workers with sensory impairments as the
receipt of communication. An obvious and important point is that communication is a two-way process. What then is the role of new technology in the
production of communication?

The enhanced ability to communicate with colleagues and employers was
cited mainly by those with hearing and speech impairments, and to a lesser
extent by workers with visual impairments, who were more inclined to focus
on the receipt of communication. This is explained in a general comment
made by Mary, a sports motivator with a severe speech impairment:

> Computers have enabled me to do a lot. This gives me a lot of confi-
> dence in writing to newspapers, and developing my writing more gen-
> erally. Also in the last couple of years I've realized that I could use
> computers to do more education. I can decide what I want to do, for
> example an OU degree in the future. I can produce letters and training
> materials more easily with a computer. I often send my comments in
> advance of meetings so that the chair can read them. This means I can
> make my point more quickly in the meeting itself. I used to use a
> manual typewriter, but I found that this was tiring and hard to control. I
> do sometimes press keys for too long on the word processor, but I use
> the spell check to put them right.
>
> (Mary, part-time sports development officer and access officer,
> wheelchair user, cerebral palsy; attitude and environmental barriers)

Here, Mary sees benefits not simply in terms of computer-aided text communication as an alternative to speech, but perceives the benefits in the
wider sense of what she is able to do with that ability. Mary admitted that
once alternatives to speech had been possible, she took the new medium for
granted, but while considering how she could use computer-based communication, she took a step back to muse on just what computers had allowed
her to communicate:

> I use computers to enable me to do the paperwork, and to do the data-
> bases for my sports development work. I couldn't do without it; basic-
> ally being able to write in a way that is legible, it puts me on a more
> equal footing. I do find that I try to impress on people what I can do.
> People often assume I have no abilities when they meet me. They
> assume that having CP makes me mentally slow, which I'm not. I sup-
> pose the computer means I can make an impression before people have
> time to form their own.
>
> (Mary)

The question of computer-based communication was also important for
Stewart, a worker with a hearing impairment, who although experiencing
negative attitudes at work, felt that computers allowed him to choose
between computer-based text or spoken communication:

Computers do allow me to communicate, and express my ability through the text rather than through the spoken word. I often choose to make my point by computer as the personal side of communication can often get in the way, and I think that, say, an e-mail message is more likely to be treated for what it is than for who is sending it. I would like to think that this won't stop people rethinking their attitudes towards me. But I don't have that luxury at the moment. At least with computerized communication I think I get more equal consideration, that my suggestions get taken more seriously.

> (Stewart, programmer, hearing impairment;
> attitude, environmental and technical barriers)

An earlier point mentioned the need to distinguish between two forms of communication, the immediate and the expressive forms. It is clear from Stewart's comments above that these benefits are often inseparable in practice. But what of the specific references to expressive communication?

Enabling expressive communication

A more direct example of the notion of expressive communication – that is, communication as an expression of abilities – was evident in Clive's comments. Clive has faced severe employment discrimination because his cerebral palsy is seen as 'unsuited' to employment by many employers. He has recently, and for the first time, had some of his abilities recognized with the advent of new technology, which has given him access to print and to computers:

> I am aware that it [new technology] may allow me to say something about my ability to those who don't realize what I am capable of. There have been a number of examples of local firms asking me to work once they are aware of my abilities. Some were obviously surprised at what I could do. I've shattered a few myths about cerebral palsy I think. The difficulty is getting those abilities over as soon as possible in the process. I think that using IT has meant that I can express my skills and expertise more quickly.
>
> (Clive, self-employed computer consultant, athetoid cerebral palsy, wheelchair user; attitude and environmental barriers)

The likelihood of a participant mentioning the communication of abilities was higher in the instances where impairment had been obvious, and where according to the disabled participant, it had shaped the attitudes of employers. Here, the communication of abilities stemmed from the disabled person's felt need to shatter stereotypes about their abilities. This was certainly true of both Mary and Clive, who both faced major discrimination as people with cerebral palsy. For them, new technology allows both the choice of a non-speech form of communication and the ability to communicate skills in a way that attempts to bypass the mechanisms of prejudice and discrimination. Clive sums up this potential benefit succinctly:

> Computers give me confidence, I feel less disabled. I have a more positive attitude to myself as the computer constantly informs me of what I'm capable of, in a way that my speech and writing doesn't. I feel that I've reached a higher plane with new technology and only hope that employers latch on to this eventually.
>
> (Clive)

This form of communicating abilities is an example of how benefits appeared to apply for different types of impairment, affecting something as fundamental as enhanced self-perception, as is evidenced in the comments of Gordon and Paul, both of whom have physical impairments but no sensory impairments:

> I work better with a machine than anything else, that is where I'm at my most able. It provides me with some extra confidence, there have been times where I have been able to advise others on technology. I use a laptop on my adapted chair. I suppose it makes me look even more different, but I spend a lot of time on the PC as it's with me most of the time. I suppose it was inevitable that I'd become good at certain things like spreadsheets, document handling and accounts software.
>
> (Gordon, finance officer, spina bifida, wheelchair user;
> attitude and environmental barriers)

> I do feel that computers allow me to express in an obvious way my abilities. Even though I admit I did not enter computer work with this as a conscious aim. I just discovered this possibility by accident. It's like a lot of things in life, you just happen to hit on something that is good for you. I have found this a number of times in my working life. The first discovery was that home correspondence teaching was well suited to me as a disabled person, I did this when I lived in New Zealand. The same has been true of working with computers. I not only use them in my work, but I design them here at Resco Machines.
>
> (Paul, systems engineer and technical author, spinal cord injury,
> uses crutches; environmental barriers)

Despite the cross-impairment nature of the personal communication of abilities, and also the straddling of such communication across computer work and technology work, there is one thread that seems to link those who reported such a dual communication function of new technology: severity of impairment. This suggests that level of impairment may be an important variable in predicting the importance of expressive communication. In sum, those with visible or severe impairments were more likely to report the function of new technology in communicating abilities. This has implications for the policy points to be discussed later in Part 3 of this work.

Conclusion

This chapter has provided clear evidence of the benefits of new technology in disabled people's working lives. It also conveys the validity and strength of adopting a social barriers approach to our understanding of these benefits. Disabled people had little difficulty connecting with this model of benefits, mentioning in each instance the barriers they face and the way in which new technology had allowed the redefinition of at least some of these barriers. However, a close reading of these perceptions of benefits also suggests that barriers still pervade the working lives of disabled people. Only in a small number of instances was it felt that barriers had been substantially and permanently erased by new technology use.

Employment environments continue to present barriers to workers and job seekers with impairments. Additionally, the potential benefits of new technology were only as great as the support provided by colleagues, employers, technology providers and policy makers. In a number of instances barriers to getting employment remained a substantial block to enabling work with new technology, even for highly skilled unemployed disabled people. In another instance, new technology was adopted in a way that led to a severe exacerbation of an inflammatory impairment, putting paid to a disabled person's long-term career prospects.

Clearly, the human element and the attitudes, practices and environments of disabled people continue to limit the enabling potential of new technology. Sadly, the shameful walls of exclusion and restriction seem still to pervade many of the employment and job-seeking experiences of disabled people. This is an appropriate point to begin to examine these continued barriers.

 **9**

Resilient barriers: continued limits to enabling technology

The previous chapter's discussion of the benefits of new technology, while suggesting its clear potential in the lives of disabled workers, should be read in conjunction with the continued barriers cited by the majority of disabled people researched. What were the remaining barriers to enabling employment? How significant were these barriers? We begin by asking a pivotal question: was evidence of continued barriers the result of the technical limits of new technology, the adverse effects of human agency; their disabling attitudes, or wider physical barriers in the workplace? Findings suggest that it would be wrong to try to identify one causal factor which continues to present barriers to an enabling workplace. All of these factors were cited by disabled participants as limiting the potential for enabling work. In line with broader findings, the following barriers were identified as continuing to limit the enabling use of new technology in the workplace: environmental, technological and attitude/structural barriers. Because much of the perceived potential of new technology is seen to reside in its revolutionary impact on the work environment, it seems appropriate to begin by looking at the environmental barriers that still feature in disabled people's working lives.

Environmental barriers: new wine in old skins?

The extent to which environmental barriers persisted for disabled workers was generally significant; this statement, however, hides a large degree of variation in the extent of these remaining barriers. At its most extreme, environmental barriers were still so significant that they continued in many instances to discount work with new technology. At the other extreme, but still important, were the large number of examples of minor limitations to enabling work caused by thoughtless working practices. The most commonly cited limitation to the full use of technological potential was the unnecessary duplication of work with both computerized and manual systems. The following comments sum up this negation of the benefits of new technology by such a duplication of effort:

As time passes we will be using the PC for more and more functions, although we keep manual records of everything.You see my supervisor has been there 30 years, and she says as long as she's there a manual back-up will stay. If I had a choice in the matter I would use the PC for all of my paperwork, except signing dockets etc., where a pen is still necessary. You see, I can see much more mileage in the machine than I'm allowed to get out. My boss has the final say in these things. My disability doesn't get recognized in this respect.

> (Jane, purchasing officer, polio, uses sticks; attitude and environmental barriers)

Similar comments came from Susan and Denise, purchasing officers who use both manual and computerized systems:

Some records are kept in folders that are above your head, when they get full they get heavy, so if it wasn't necessary to use the hard copy it would be better. As I say, when we first got the system, managers encouraged us [supervisors and clerical workers] to transfer everything to our computers. There were two problems with this: the cost of them, especially when they went wrong, and some staff lost work initially. From that point we have kept a number of documents in manual form. This obviously makes things physically much harder. It means that the savings of the computer are lost to me on occasions. Actually invoices are the biggest problem, we still receive billings in paper form, so most of these are processed manually.

> (Denise, purchasing office supervisor, hemiplegia; environmental barriers)

And similarly:

At work we have a suspended filing system and I cannot use it because my arms are not strong enough to get files out. I have to rely on others. I cannot understand why we don't just use the computers, that's what they got them for.

> (Susan, purchasing officer, rheumatoid arthritis; attitude and environmental barriers)

Here, it is possible to see how in Jane, Denise and Susan's work, the duplication of practices can lead to a negation of the energy-saving potential of new technology, and to the continued dependence of disabled workers on non-disabled colleagues. An increased confidence in the security of computerized records may lead to a gradual withdrawal from paper-based office practices. Unfortunately, despite prognostications of the paperless office (Gill 1985: 19), there is little evidence that employers are willing to go the whole way in this process (Tenner 1988: 29). Bills, invoices, dockets, application forms, standing orders and legal documents are still predominantly generated, processed, filed and retrieved in manual forms, despite the parallel existence of a computer record. Clearly, the decision to retain manual records is likely to take priority over the question of accessible and user-friendly working environments for a disabled workforce.

Even for those computer workers using new technology as the focus of their work, physical barriers can still loom large. Here the question of 'configured' barriers, a recurrent theme in this study, is supported by the following comments from workers with arthritis:

> Conventional dials, knobs and controls all present problems; the office complex was not designed with disabled people in mind. The building I'm now in was built in the 1980s but was not made with disabled people in mind. It would be expensive but nice, to have a building that had lifts and a more 'hi-tech' environment that had electronic doors. There is a lift, but it's a goods lift with a pull-by-hand concertina door, which is completely impossible for me. It would be nicer to have an easy-to-use environment.
>
> (Ray, computer services manager, rheumatoid arthritis; environmental barriers)

Similarly:

> It's the toilets, they are not fully adapted, they have tried to help by putting handles around the toilet, but they didn't ask me exactly what I wanted. This is the low point in my work, as I dread using the toilets, they are unmanageable for me.
>
> (Val, senior personal secretary, rheumatoid arthritis; environmental barriers)

Here evidence of configured physical barriers crosses over the computer worker (Ray) and technology user (Val) categories. What is significant is that although a range of workers were subject to configured barriers, the more senior the disabled person was in the occupational hierarchy, generally the more confident they were about changing physical barriers. Conversely, those disabled workers in relatively low status positions were less sanguine about changing environments. As Ray comments,

> I do still face barriers in my work as I've said, but as a [middle] manager I have a certain degree of influence in getting things changed. Now the wheels turn slowly at the best of times, but I think that if I put my mind to it I could get changes to door handles and maybe certain heavy doors in this part of the office complex. I am less certain about the lift, as that would inevitably require a five-figure sum for an upgrade to a passenger lift. But I'm lucky that if I needed to pull out the stops I could, I've been here a long time. I suppose I might have said more before, but even as a manager, I worry that it might turn the spotlight on me.
>
> (Ray, computer services manager, rheumatoid arthritis; environmental barriers)

This seems to suggest that attitude barriers are still embedded in the organization in which Ray works, but that they may operate in differing ways according to the status of the employee. Interestingly, Ray felt that environmental barriers were the only significant barrier he faced at the time. Jane provides a very contrasting image to Ray. As a clerical-grade worker she admitted that she was quite powerless to effect enabling changes in her workplace:

Initially I mentioned that the filing system and the use of paper made my job more difficult. I suggested that we move to computers to make work easier. My supervisor wasn't best pleased, she felt that it wasn't her job to make work easier, but just to get the job done efficiently. I learnt to keep quiet. By speaking out about my work, how it's done, I felt that I was vulnerable; you know most people worry about losing their jobs these days. I didn't feel that I had a lot to gain by asking for a reorganization of my work, even though I can see how my work could be more 'enabling' as you put it.

(Jane, purchasing officer, polio, uses sticks; attitude and environmental barriers)

It is interesting to note how negative attitudes link with disabling environments in these experiences, and show that they are indeed inseparable.

Richard provides the final picture of continued environmental barriers to enabling work. The following illustrates how the environmental layout of an office can shape how new technology is used. Richard, a principal planning officer with advanced multiple sclerosis, uses new technology substantially to access his wider working environment, with most of his work being done on his PC and a personal electronic notetaker. Unfortunately, Richard's work is not ideally suited to his changing condition:

I haven't got room on my desk for a PC so I have it on the table behind me. It is about 6–8 feet away. I have to go from place to place, it can be very frustrating having to do this, and I feel that I waste energy every time I move over to the PC. I use the PC for almost everything, I even take notes on an electronic notetaker which allows me to transpose these straight on to a floppy disk. This way there's less paper involved. I have asked if I could have a desk elsewhere. Unfortunately space is at a premium as colleagues need the space to produce and alter plans, which requires acres of space for each planner. I cannot help feel that my work would be ten times better if I had just one workstation. I know this because I work for part of my week at home and I know how much easier it is to function at one desk. I suppose that working at home means that I have even less influence over office space as I'm not as much a part of the furniture than I was. Ironically, we planners are constrained by the fact that we need a larger office, but can't get one. Because Oxport is a historic place, the planning bit is made even more restrictive, even for professional planners.

(Richard, principal planning officer, multiple sclerosis, wheelchair user; attitude and environmental barriers)

Although a principal planning officer, Richard is not on the management spine of planning officers and therefore has little clout in his organization, and as he notes, there are wider factors that constrain the choices over the use of office space.

The above examples amply demonstrate how near some disabled workers are to enabling technology and enabling work. They also illustrate the simple and in many instances low cost measures that could be introduced to help create enabling environments more fully. Another identifiable form of barrier which forms part of this configuration is technical barriers, barriers belonging to the technology itself.

Technological barriers

Technological barriers should be seen as a varied, sometimes contradictory set of limitations to enabling working environments. In sum, technological barriers can be divided into two discrete forms. Firstly, some barriers stem from the qualities of technologies themselves. The examples of computer graphics and visual display more generally are barriers for some workers. The second form of technological barrier relates to the culture that surrounds the use of technology. Here issues in rapid technological change, incompatibility of hard- and software, and the intensive nature of technology use came out of the research findings.

What then of these technological barriers? We can begin with the first type mentioned. It may seem extraordinary, given the promise of new technology, that certain technological applications (hardware and software) are potentially limiting. However, a small number of participants, mainly those with visual impairments, were sceptical about an unalloyed faith in the value of new technology. Participants with visual impairments cited examples of what were, for most workers, clear advances in working methods, but which created problems for them.

Particular problems attached to the increased use of computer graphics. The use of screen icons, desktop-published documents and graphics-dominated computing packages were all cited as problems for workers with visual impairments. The use of Optacons, screen readers, Braille and speech output devices were all to some extent negated by the growth in graphics, as these specialized technologies had been produced to enhance alphabetical text access. Graphics are not ordinarily intelligible to such access technologies.

Workers with visual impairments, many of whom were computer analysts and programmers, mentioned their immediate problems in accessing documents, alongside their concern that computer graphics may increasingly dominate personal computer use. After benefiting from more access to computer-based text, the prospect of losing this access and hard-won computing skills to graphics was a bleak one.

It was clear from talking to workers with visual impairments that changes in working technologies were experienced as a series of mixed developments, with steps forward in accessible technologies being paralleled by retrograde developments. Here William, an unemployed computer programmer with a visual impairment, reflects on his experience of technological change from reliance on mainframes and punch card operation to desktop visual display units:

I was excellent on punch cards. We switched over [to VDUs] when we got the 2904 and 2960. That was a VDU-based computer and was more difficult because the screens were not that brilliant. I was spending three or four times as long as other people doing the same sort of thing at the keyboard. The VDU input put me at a disadvantage at first, and I had to use my hand lens and scan the screen by hand. Very laborious. I really did feel as though I'd be left behind by this use of the VDU. I mean, eventually I became good with VDUs and screen-based working but that wasn't my initial experience.
(William, unemployed programmer, visual impairment; attitude, environmental and technical barriers)

Here William's tactile experience of punch cards was suddenly rendered redundant by the rapid and imposed shifts to VDUs. Particularly negative experiences were identified by workers who had applied for and received specialized technology. Here barriers were those of difficulty in using a specific technology, and also the inherently poor and stigmatizing design of some technologies. The commonest example given was that of closed circuit television (CCTV). Here the size and cumbersome nature of CCTVs provoked the following comments:

Can I tell you one thing, I've got a closed circuit television, but it's very clumsy to use. They work on an x/y pedestal (like a microfiche); to use it you have to be aware of your position on the grid, it's easy to get lost, it's quicker to read close and not bother to use the CCTV.
(Tony, computer services manager, visual impairment; technical barriers)

William had also found CCTV use very difficult. Here he explains why he thinks the CCTV has not been useful for many visually impaired workers:

Devices which in principle benefit the visually impaired, such as the closed circuit television, have been manufactured to make a 'quick buck'; it is an abuse of technology in that it has been designed to have the scan and view functions in one piece, inseparable. This means that it puts the price up to £2000. The much cheaper approach would be to have the TV part separate from the grid. This would make it transportable, and could be used at home or the office. Someone sees a niche in the market, but never asks the questions of the people who might use it.
(William, unemployed programmer, visual impairment; attitude, environmental and technical barriers)

William's comment not only indicates the possible negative impetus behind some specialized technologies, but is a clear endorsement of the assertion that many disabled people are experts in assessing their employment and technology needs. In this instance a piece of technology is less than ideal for some workers because it has been designed with little if any consideration of what disabled people want.

A number of people with visual impairments noted the still primitive nature of some new technology, and that some potentially revolutionary technologies were still technically short of their full potential. For example speech synthesis, a specialized output technology, was mentioned on two occasions by workers with visual impairments as too primitive to attract wholesale interest. Here are some examples:

> The speech output on my jotta [integrated computer with specialized input/output] has limited words and has a mechanical articulation. Designers I know are working to improve the clarity of the speech and want to make it less embarrassing, but I am amazed that anyone ever agrees to use speech output. The tone and speed of the speech is enough to make you cringe. I might sound ungrateful, but designers sometimes forget that we have to use the system in public, it can make you self-conscious; and I am not what you might call 'shy and retiring' by nature.
>
> (Trevor, programmer, visual impairment;
> attitude, environmental and technical barriers)

William's comments on his experiences of speech synthesizers are a variation on this theme:

> The biggest problem I've encountered are voice synthesizers; they range from Metal Mickey to ... the voices are very bad, very tinny, always American. One of the systems, I just couldn't understand a word.
>
> (William, unemployed programmer, visual impairment;
> attitude, environmental and technical barriers)

The main difference here between the CCTV and the speech synthesizer is that although they are both primitive, the speech synthesizer is viewed as basically sound but needing further development, whereas the CCTV in its present form is seen as inherently misguided and not referenced to the need of workers with impairments. This does not discount the value to some workers of CCTV, but suggests that consultation and choice are paramount in the process of conception, design and testing of all potentially beneficial technologies.

The second group of examples in the research, of technology-related barriers, concerned the 'culture' of new technology. What is meant by the cultural barriers to enabling technology use? Evidence suggests that the very revolution in working methods made possible by the integrated circuit may itself also encourage activities that are hostile to the enabling of disabled workers. Here 'culture' is made up of an amalgam of organizational, technical and gender assumptions about new technology and how it can be used. The intention of this focus is not to explore in any detail these cultural assumptions but to look at how participants identified barriers in these terms.

Organizational culture, technological change and gender

This research has not uncovered widespread evidence of new technology being used to intensify work practices; indeed its findings generally support Child's notion of 'social choice' in the way technology is used (in Knights and Willmott 1985). Social choice theory suggests that there are diverse reasons for introducing new technology which make universalist explanations misleading. However, this research has found that a small number of junior clerical staff, particularly disabled female workers, noted an increased intensity of work with the advent of new technologies. This was far less likely to be the reported experience of disabled male workers, regardless of their employment status.

While the literature on the organizational objectives of introducing new technology is inconclusive and conflicting (see Cockburn 1983, 1985; Thompson 1983; Daniel 1987); what seems to be clear is the heightened susceptibility of women, especially lower status, white-collar workers to more intensive, less controllable work with new technology (see Cockburn 1983, 1985; Harvey in Lee and Loveridge 1987; Crompton and Sanderson 1990: 123–24).

More research needs to be done to establish the significance of employment status and gender in shaping disabled people's experiences of new technology. It is possible, however, to maintain tentatively that assumptions about lower status office work suggest that employers may be adopting new technology in a way that aims to maximize returns on its use. This claim, if it is correct, suggests that already vulnerable and relatively powerless workers may benefit least from the planned enabling use of new technology. This point is borne out in the following comments from disabled women in junior clerical work:

I thought that with new technologies my work would get easier. I had heard how user-friendly they were, and had felt the soft touch keyboards. As my MS was quite bad at the time they were introduced I thought the quality of my work would improve, and my job. I was wrong, the computers were introduced very quickly, with little technical or training support; it was sink or swim. Anyway, secretaries didn't get priority access. The most striking thing for me was that our line managers expected us all to work even harder; we were told the computer could calculate how many letters typists and secretaries had done. I don't know to this day whether that is true, but it certainly meant those who did get access to the machines worked even harder.

(Joan, part-time secretary, multiple sclerosis; attitude, environmental and technical barriers)

Joan felt that the advent of more powerful and user-friendly technologies had made available more intensive methods of working. She felt that her employers assumed she would do more work with the new technology. Here the organizational impetus behind the adoption of new technologies seemed to revolve around the perception of new technology increasing efficiencies, efficiencies that would be repaid in terms of increased throughput of work. Margaret makes a similar point when discussing the broader organizational changes word processors instigated:

> When the VDUs [PCs] were introduced they decided to go all audio. Well I don't like audio typing, it is easy and effective as a technique, but I found that it was as though nothing else existed except his voice and my fingers really. Before then I was using an electric and doing shorthand, the little breaks meant all the difference. I think my boss saw how easy the machines were to operate and assumed they would make audio work more acceptable. Initially, I was quite keen on the idea of using a word processor, my friends had one and I found the keyboards so easy to use. Unfortunately my boss didn't advise me on the necessary breaks you have to take to avoid strains. The technology was so easy to use it led me into a false sense of security. When my boss told me I had to leave I felt against the VDUs [PCs].
>
> (Margaret, unemployed secretary, psoriatic arthropathy;
> attitude, environmental and technical barriers)

Margaret felt that new technology gave her employer an excuse to alter her employment tasks more generally. Unfortunately, not only did this lead to more intensive use of the personal computer, but it also led to deteriorating health, and to her eventual unemployment. The danger, especially as in Margaret's experience where a disabled person is employed in a small organization, is that technology may be used in a way that impairs some workers, especially where pay-back and efficiency concerns override the issue of the quality of working life. Fortunately this intensification of work was mentioned by only two of the 30 disabled people interviewed, both of whom worked in small businesses. However, the dynamics that led to such misuse of technology can be seen to have a wider significance, one that must be accounted for in any assessment of the likely impact of new technology on disabled workers.

Another theme which came out of the research which could broadly be encapsulated in the notion of 'lack of adequate support' was that of training. A fifth of the interview group (6) reported inadequate training in new technology use. This was seen as a problem for all workers new to personal computer work. For disabled employees the impact was even more stark:

> Initially I thought we would get a lot from them [PCs]. This has not been realized as much as I thought it might be. With training we could get a lot more out of them. When you have a lot of people without training, you can easily be using the computer for the wrong reasons,

and end up doing something that is more long-winded than the manual system. Conversely, this lack of training might mean that many disabled workers don't know the labour-saving features in the software.

(Susan, purchasing officer, rheumatoid arthritis;
attitude and environmental barriers)

The lack of training, poor training and lack of familiarization with PC working meant that a number of disabled workers (6) felt threatened by the terminology that pervades personal computer use. The implications of this were significant, if short-lived:

In the early stages, a lot of the time, I didn't know what people were talking about, with the terminology: megabytes and so on.you could get used to the feel of the language, but you didn't really understand what it was because there was far too much to learn. I think some guidance on which terms were essential, which were less important would have been very useful. I think the computer people, usually young men, assume you know more than you do.

(Denise, purchasing officer, hemiplegia;
attitude and environmental barriers)

A related point made by Richard, suggests that the frustration with the culture of new technology is not explicable in terms of a gendering of the language, one where men were always unfairly advantaged:

I was rather resentful of the mystique attached to them [computers]. I suspected it was all a con, that they were not that mysterious. Through my own efforts I have found out that they are not. It seemed odd when desktop computing became more common, it's as if the experts wanted us all to use them, but didn't want us knowing *too much* about them as this might impact on their power and mystique.

(Richard, senior planning officer, multiple sclerosis, wheelchair user;
attitude and environmental barriers)

Richard's sentiments seem to capture in lay terms much of the sociological literature on professional projects and the power of linguistic obfuscation and exclusive 'cultural work' in cementing occupational power and autonomy (Pettigrew 1975; Freidson 1986; MacDonald 1995:163–7).

New technology, change and the permanent revolution

Another aspect of the research findings that can best be placed under the rubric of 'culture' is that of the rapid nature of technological change. Here the culture of new technology production, redesign, upgrading and obsolescence was seen by some as inimical to a fully enabling use of new technology. Again, no attempt will be made to explore the exact reasons for this culture of permanent technological revolution; it is noteworthy, however, that the effects of this were mentioned by a significant minority (10 out of 30), and were couched in terms of the uncontrollability of technical change, the difficulty of keeping up with these changes, and (most significantly) the incompatibility of systems that result from such changes. What is clear from the findings is that the speed of (mainstream) technological change is out of the control of disabled and able-bodied workers. What is significant for some disabled workers is that their reliance on new technology to open up the employment domain makes them more susceptible to the effects of rapid technological change. As Ahmed points out:

> My work involves a lot of word processing, compiling reports and constructing user guides for staff to use. The speed that software packages change is phenomenal. If you don't have the latest package it's easy to feel left behind. I'm fortunate in liking PC work and see the changes as a challenge. I even do some work at home to keep up with the changes in software. But I can imagine that for some workers, they haven't got the time, energy or inclination to update their use of word processing packages. This can be a problem if you find work tiring. It can seem like an unnecessary toil to keep up sometimes.
>
> (Ahmed, computer officer, spinal cord injury, wheelchair user; attitude, environmental and technical barriers)

Perhaps the most worrying organizational response to technological developments was evidenced in the experiences of Steve, a graphic designer and artist with multiple sclerosis. Steve had been doing manual artwork, but because of his deteriorating multiple sclerosis found that he would benefit from computerized graphics. He had dabbled with computer-generated graphics and felt that his work would be much more controllable using keyboard commands than brush and pencil work. Even though Steve wanted to make the transfer to computerized art production he was effectively supplanted by the technology as his employers decided to make him redundant. Interestingly, his manager couched the reasons for his redundancy in terms of the new requirements of computerized graphics, suggesting that Steve no longer had the most appropriate skills to be employed with the new technology:

> It [graphic design/art] became more technically innovative, more computers were added. Towards the end they had three Apple Mac workstations. The job was moving away from illustration/design to more pagemaking and layout. In that way I was being supplanted by the technology, they had some very good keyboard artists so I was left out to some degree. I was always conscious that the computers were coming. I always wanted to use them. I was saddened that I never really got a proper chance to use them when it mattered. I never really got the chance to see how new technology could help with my physical ability to work.
>
> (Steve, unemployed graphic designer, multiple sclerosis, uses sticks; attitude, environmental and technical barriers)

The outcome of technical and organizational change was particularly harsh for Steve, as it was for Margaret. Their experiences of new technology and employment change represent a worst-case scenario, where enabling potential is overshadowed by a disabling use of new technology. Nevertheless, similarities can be drawn between Steve and Margaret's experiences and the more general experiences of the majority of technology workers in this study. The common factor linking all of these was the unnegotiated character of technological change. Clearly, for the majority of disabled people this was not inherently a negative experience. However, the benefits of new technology for this group were fortuitous rather than planned. Organizational and technical change simply fitted with the basic preferences and rarely acknowledged needs of disabled workers. Such unplanned use, and the absence of disabled workers' voices in the process of change, led to an inevitable mix of enabling and disabling consequences. It is not difficult to see how the absence of disabled people's voices and preferences at times of technological change is rooted in deeper attitudes. It is to these attitude barriers that we now turn.

Attitudes: the master barrier?

The findings on barriers suggests that attitudes are at some point connected to more specific environmental and technological barriers. Indeed it is sometimes difficult to separate out any discrete influence of attitudes barriers. The following analysis addresses the range of attitude barriers disabled workers reported. What forms, then, did attitude barriers take? We can distinguish between the *source* and *effects* of attitude barriers. In terms of the *source* of barriers, three basic agents were identified:

1 *employers*, the main source of attitude barriers;
2 *colleagues*, a less commonly cited source of negative attitudes;
3 *professionals*, a common source of negative attitudes and effects where specialized technology was provided.

Because many participants cited the same attitude barriers stemming from more than one source, it was also important to see attitudes in terms of their *effects*. Here we can divide attitudes into:

• *General attitudes and effects* – taken to mean the effects of historical and cultural attitudes that have shaped the experiences of disabled workers or job seekers. Here direct effects varied, but were the result of negative assumptions about disabled people's employment abilities and limitations.
• *Attitudes limiting acquisition* – a common experience, one where access to new technology was limited by employers unwilling to acknowledge the benefits of technology; by Disablement Advisory Service officials dictating the special aids 'needs' of disabled workers; and colleague antipathy to disabled workers receiving technology that was not available to able-bodied workers.

• *Attitudes that limit enabling technology use* – here again colleague and employer attitudes were seen to link with disabling acts, such as intransigence, demarcation, cultural and organizational exclusion. The effect of these attitudes was to limit the potential of new technology for disabled workers, even where significant use of new technology was made by disabled employees.

General attitudes

About half of the interviewees expressed barriers in terms of the primacy of disabling attitudes. Many of these highlighted major attitude problems that they continued to face in their work, or less commonly in their search for work. The most worrying comments referred to the process of excluding workers with severe impairments from employment by associating physical impairment with intellectual inadequacy. Even when employment was obtained, employers underestimated some disabled workers' abilities. This was seen as limiting career advancement, in promotion for example. The first of these examples of grossly stereotyped disabling attitudes were experienced by Clive and Mary.

Clive has cerebral palsy and is well qualified in the use of new technology after ten years' experience of spreadsheet and database work. At the time of interview he was continuing his protracted search for more work to bolster his part-time work of five to ten hours per month. Clive felt that based on previous experience, he could work up to 35 hours per week. Clive felt that the main barrier to more IT work was unfavourable employer perceptions of people with cerebral palsy:

> Employers are prejudiced against those with CP, and also against those in wheelchairs.You can tell by the expression on their face.They also assume that because my speech is impaired I'm mentally handicapped. That hurts. I've been for a number of jobs where I've not stated on the application form that I have CP, and have had some interviews. Employers seem amazed that I would even have the nerve to go for a job with my disabilities. I feel that what I say only confirms what they already think.They have already got this mental picture of what I'm capable of.You could say you were a world expert on database construction, but it wouldn't make a bit of difference.
>
> (Clive, part-time database and spreadsheet worker, cerebral palsy, wheelchair user; attitude and environmental barriers)

Mary reports similar experiences. She too had ample experience of software applications when she applied for a job with the CP Society as microtechnology officer. Even though she had been trained by the Society, and although the job was exactly what she had been trained to do, the job went to a non-disabled worker:

I applied for a job as a microtechnology officer. It was basically the same job as the software researcher [the job she was doing when applying], but it was training other disabled people to use technology. But it was decided that I didn't have enough experience for the job, the major problem was that the CP Society wasn't ready to employ a severely disabled person and didn't know how to go about it. I couldn't believe the Society's attitudes in employing an able-bodied person ahead of a person with cerebral palsy. One great asset people with CP have is an insider knowledge of what it's like. As the job I went for was training others with CP to use new technology, I could offer unique personal experience. I look back with frustration on this. The Society has changed, but even one experience of this kind was pretty devastating for me. I had to accept that the Society at the time contradicted itself, on the one hand saying how capable we [people with CP] all are, and on the other refusing to employ people with CP.

> (Mary, part-time sports development worker, cerebral palsy,
> wheelchair user; attitude and environmental barriers)

This effective writing-off of ability was also reported by participants when discussing the role of disablement resettlement officers in their attempts to find work. In three instances, DRO staff labelled participants 'unemployable'. For those labelled this was devastating, and effectively the basis of a self-fulfilling barrier. Here, disabled job seekers admitted that for some time they had explained their unemployment in terms of their unemployability, rather than in terms of disabling employer attitudes. This DRO labelling of disabled people as unemployable is hard evidence of the deficit model of disability in operation; this is astounding, given that the labellers of the 'unemployable' are paid to enhance employment opportunities.

The underestimation of ability, even where disabled workers had significant technology skills and experiences, also continued into employment itself. Perhaps the most common expression of this came in those comments that referred to limited promotion prospects. A number of workers referred to this underrating of ability and subsequent denial of promotion opportunities. Here are some representative examples:

The problem is that employers have fairly fixed ideas about your capabilities. They read that off from looking at you. That is, you don't appear to them as dynamic as you may be. This is the difficulty, you don't *appear* to have the get-up-and-go, in employers' eyes. My line manager sees me struggle to walk, he assumes that I struggle with everything. It's odd really, they [managers] seem to go by appearances more than anything else. Yet I've got colleagues who are not disabled who don't work as productively as I do, and who take loads of time off; but managers don't seem to look at them in the same way. It's assumed that they don't struggle to do work. In promotion terms, you do have to work hard to get to senior status say, but it's not just that, you have to have this aura of efficiency and drive that many disabled people don't have. It's all a bit of a con. Actually the term 'get up and go' is a telling one, especially if like me you use walking sticks.

>   (Roland, word processor, polio, uses sticks;
>   attitude and environmental barriers)

The result of these attitudes, ones that conflate appearance with reality, ideology with ability, are also borne out in the following comments about promotion opportunities:

As a blind programmer I am aware of the different treatment in, say, promotion. I don't think it completely debars promotion, but in my case it has made it much more difficult. I think there's a tendency for supervisors to remember the problems encountered with blind colleagues, rather than, say, my achievements. I also think that being blind or visually handicapped [impaired] isn't seen as suited to leadership roles. I'm probably not as ambitious as some of my colleagues, but as ambitious as most of them in programming.

>   (Graham, programmer, blind;
>   attitude, environmental and technical barriers)

Edward makes a similar point:

Most of the time at the DSE [anonymized name] I have felt I have wasted my time. I have tried several times to get to executive officer because that's the grade you have to be if you want to do computer work. I am never going to be able to do the job I want, it's a kind of rejection. I personally think that bosses are no different to anyone else. They have the same prejudices and hang-ups. Being hard of hearing I feel that I get treated with contempt. My immediate boss is flabbergasted that I should put in for EO promotion, and that I should be as persistent. I don't honestly think that I would still be an AO if I was hearing. Personally I don't think of the exact reasons why I haven't been promoted. I think that would make me too angry. I just know I'm not the only deaf person in the DSE who has failed to get promotion, even though they have tried many times.

>   (Edward, administrative officer, hearing impairment;
>   attitude, environmental and technical barriers)

Other attitudes that may have contributed to this emphasis on inabilities (rather than abilities) were identified. Pity, existential discomfort and aesthetic shock (see Oliver 1990) all seemed to play their part in this construction of disabled workers' identities. Here are examples of each of the above attitudes:

On pity:

The boss I have at the moment is very young, she's 24, a high flier, when she sees me helping Janet [another disabled employee], and I use my teeth to help put her coat on, she looks with amazement. She once said:

'When I look at you and Janet it makes me feel so lucky.' I'm old enough to ignore these sorts of comments; Janet is less tolerant, she has had a few run-ins with this boss over her attitude. From my point of view I just want to blend in here, I'm not looking for pity, I mean pity is just not something I can comprehend now as I've had this [hemiplegia] for so long I don't think about it for 99 per cent of the time. It's only when I'm reminded of it, usually by staff that are new to EAA [anonymized name]. Frankly, most staff don't make an issue of it.

(Denise, purchasing officer, hemiplegia;
attitude and environmental barriers)

On existential discomfort:

I have got one [boss] now who just cannot come to terms with having a blind secretary, she doesn't like me 'doing the doing'. She cannot seem to accept that I'm happy being a blind secretary. She's relatively new, and I don't think she's worked with someone with a sight problem. She keeps asking for reassurance that I'm alright. Why shouldn't I be, I have been working for 20 years before she even qualified as a social worker.

(Mandy, secretary to social worker, blind;
attitude and environmental barriers)

On aesthetic shock:

If I went for a job with six able-bodied girls. I am unlikely to get the job. People go by appearance, they want someone 'presentable' to meet people, the hospitality bit. I know this because in the early days I went for a number of jobs. Employers then were quite upfront about their preferences, and I could tell they were surprised that I was putting in for often high profile PA jobs even though I do not look like a typical PA. It's a sort of unwritten rule that PAs should be glamorous, tall and all appearance. I could never live up to that, but I felt that I might eventually get a boss who chose staff on the basis of what they could do, not how they looked. It meant that I have had to lower my sights over the years and work my way up the secretarial ladder. However, I eventually found a managing director here who valued my work, and I'm a successful PA. But if I was to go for PA jobs elsewhere I think the response would still be one of surprise.

(Val, senior personal secretary, polyarthritis;
attitude and environmental barriers)

The above represent the worst and perhaps most extreme forms of disabling attitudes; ones that in some instances severely limit the employment options of the participants concerned. Perhaps the most disturbing attitudes reported were those that led to grossly discriminatory and insensitive work practices. Two examples of gross discrimination came out of this study.

The first concerns Richard's attempt to obtain a parking space closer to his office, and the opposition he faced. Richard, a principal planning officer, has mobility limitations and reported being hampered by a disabling workplace. A major problem related to the car parking facilities at his workplace which meant he had to park about 300 metres away from the main entrance. In order to gain easier access to the office Richard applied for a parking space adjacent to the main entrance. Unfortunately the attitudes of senior management were not supportive, and seemed to place hierarchical status above the needs of workers with impairments, as Richard elaborates:

> When I raised the fact that I was having difficulty walking across the car park, and [asked] 'could I have a space nearer the door?' there was a lot of opposition, saying it would mean one less space for senior management. The implication was that it was outrageous that I should want to even dare ask. Although our business is planning, which includes issues of access, my managers seemed to separate off access issues in abstract, which they had to take account of in planning processes, and my own access issue. I think this is because my request directly impinged on their own space and their deep-rooted views about MS.
> (Richard, principal planning officer, multiple sclerosis, wheelchair user; attitude and environmental barriers)

Richard's experience suggests both widespread ignorance of disabled workers' needs and engrained organizational thinking on hierarchy, privilege and the low status of a disabled worker in that hierarchy. Effectively, Richard seemed to be short-circuiting this system, and soon realized the dynamics of attitude barriers. However, he eventually got his parking space after much management deliberation and some disapproval.

Ahmed's experience reflects a serious – and one might suppose unlawful – result of negative attitudes towards him as a disabled worker. He began a job as a computer officer with a geological exploration company. The attitude of his employers was to prejudge his abilities (he is a qualified geologist) and to assume that he would only do four days work against his colleagues' five. Although starting-off on a four-day contract, he was later asked to work five days. Effectively, he was employed to do the normal working week but was paid only for four:

> When I started I was contracted to do a four-day week and was paid on that basis. Later they realized they would need me five days per week. So they did, but they did not change my salary. I was only paid for four days; this is what comes of being disabled, because I knew if I said no to them I was relatively powerless. I suppose my views on this change quite dramatically; some days I just think I'm lucky to have a job given the odds against me working, other days I think, no, I'm as good as anyone else, and I should get a fair reward for what I do. But I can't escape the fact that I'm being ripped off. I'm always looking for a new job.
> (Ahmed, computer officer, spinal injury, wheelchair user; attitude and environmental barriers)

Richard and Ahmed's experiences reflect a major problem for disabled people, that of a lack of 'voice' in their working lives. Although it could be argued that many workers are powerless, disabled workers clearly face added barriers in the workplace. An example is the widespread assumption that disabled workers should feel lucky that their employers have had the heart to employ them, and that to demand parity or special provision is to abuse this good faith, to bite the outstretched hand of employers. In a sense this assumption connects with the earlier discussion of pity. Pity clearly overlaps with this paternalistic approach to employing disabled people.

Although the basic thrust of this research is one which highlights the value of new technology for disabled workers, the expression of concern by some interviewees that they may eventually forfeit choice by entering IT work demands attention. It was even suggested by one person that new technology work may become the new 'scheduled work' (the 1944 Disabled Persons (Employment) Act used the term to refer to work as a lift operator or car park attendant), an employment ghetto into which disabled workers would be channelled. What comments were made about stereotyping, and how do they relate to possible attitude barriers? A representative example was provided by Alan, a university library cataloguer:

> Being stuck as a cataloguer because of my disability and strengths with technology is a problem. I would like to do something, shall we say creative. The way I look at it, the library management may be saying:'Alan is doing a good job, and because of his disability it's going to be a problem to find him suitable work.' I think there's a danger that employers, operating in the way that they do, identify new technology with disabled workers in such a way that they [disabled people] find it increasingly difficult to get work outside of IT. It is just as important that employers get the message that disabled people want choice in the work that they do; both with and without new technology.
>
> (Alan, senior library assistant, uses walking frame, multiple sclerosis; attitude and environmental barriers)

Although Alan's choices were clearly constrained here, the relatively high status of his work, as with many of the jobs examined in this research, are a sharp contrast with the 'scheduled work' of the 1944 Disabled Persons (Employment) Act. However, the possibility of attitudes leading to such stereotyping may more narrowly reflect a broader conservatism on the part of employers to keep disabled workers in jobs in which they have established skills.

Attitudes limiting access to technology

Attitudes can make barriers to the acquisition of new technology. This was a particularly common experience for those who had applied for specialized microchip technology from the Disablement Advisory Service. The following responses are from:

- workers who were already using new technology but who had experienced major barriers in acquiring it;
- workers who had faced problems in getting additional and upgrading technology; and
- workers who were attempting to get their first piece of supportive technology.

Both employers and the Disablement Advisory Service (now part of the PACT) staff were identified as having attitudes that were barriers in the process of acquiring specialized technology. An example is given by Mandy, a blind secretary who works in a social work department:

Basically the health authority were prepared to pay a similar amount for a PC to that which they would pay out for an electronic typewriter for a sighted girl. Apart from the medical records they are not really into computers. No account was taken of the fact that new technology was then a lifeline for me. The bureaucratic farce that ensued when I asked for the PC was unbelievable. Anyone would think I'd asked for a luxury item. I explained that I had word processed before and that a PC would make a world of difference to the quality and ease of my work. My request was met with a stony silence.

(Mandy, secretary to a social worker, blind;
attitude and environmental barriers)

Not only was the hospital culture 'low-tech' at the time (mid-1980s), Mandy asked for a personal computer; but more worryingly, managers and personnel repeatedly failed to acknowledge Mandy's reasons for wanting the technology. Mandy eventually (and under her own steam) managed to begin the process of acquisition through the Royal Blind Society [RBS, anonymized] in Aylesford and the local Disablement Advisory Service. This proved to be a less than auspicious process. Mandy describes how she was kept waiting for inordinate periods of time for her application to be processed, how she was ignorant of its development, and how when it finally arrived it was not suited to her needs. The package provided reflected the needs and priorities of the Disablement Advisory Service itself; her own expertise was ignored. This is how she sums up her experience of professional attitudes:

DAS uses the RBS to assess us, because they think they know us very well, they do actually know a bit more than the DAS teams. I think the DAS teams can cope with large print screens and things like that, but they are not computer-literate themselves. The RBS adviser, after assessing my 'needs' then reported back to the DAS team. What she had put down was completely wrong, I don't think she put down one thing that I mentioned. The whole process took about a year; it involved an aptitude test, and then it was a matter of contacting the RBS. Quite honestly they didn't answer at all. If I hadn't chased them through the DAS team I don't think I'd have got it [IT] at all. There's always this reluctance, I don't know whose money they think they are spending;

they do not like you telling them what you want. They don't know a lot about computers but they think they have to have the last say.

(Mandy)

The transcript is given almost in full as it captures the range of experiences reported by most of the participants who had used the Disablement Advisory Service to acquire technology. The question of imposed needs, the over-looking of applicants' own specialist knowledge, and the begrudging air that pervades provision, characterizes a number of experiences of the Special Aids Scheme. Here are a few more comments that seem to corroborate the points Mandy makes:

> The PC finally arrived about a year after the application was placed. It was a foul-up according to DAS. I suspect the money ran out for the year, and they . . . had to wait for the next tax year. They made no effort to contact me to keep me informed of the progress of my application. This said a lot about their views towards me. I gave up the ghost, then three months later a letter arrived saying the order was complete, and that I'd soon be taking delivery of the equipment. Actually when I phoned them to firm this up, they said 'all's well that ends well'. That wasn't my view, and I told them I was unhappy with the whole process.
> (Richard, principal planning officer, multiple sclerosis, wheelchair user; attitude and environmental barriers)

> I applied [to DAS] twice, I waited 18 months for an answer and they replied saying I cannot have anything till I get a job. I was livid with DAS, they were so rude to me. Again, the usual thing – they know how severely disabled I am; everything follows on from that. I assumed at the time that some disabled people were responded to straight away, depending on their disability. I was really persistent, but there's only so much you can do when someone refuses to reply to your letters and phone calls. I think there should have been a complaints procedure.
> (Clive, part-time database and spreadsheet worker, wheelchair user, cerebral palsy; attitude and environmental barriers)

There is evidence here of a Catch-22 operating. Clive was told that he could not get support unless he had a job. Conversely, Clive felt that the odds of him getting a job without being able to take with him a package of supporting technology was very low. This seems to confirm the reservations raised about the SAE scheme in Chapter 5 above, and presents a serious barrier to what is supposed to be *aids to* employment.

A small number of comments suggested that workers may on occasion have been trapped between a begrudging employer and DAS officials. Here is Mandy again, this time at the point at which she had begun to approach the DAS for new technology support:

> I kept getting nil response [to the application] or 'no, you can't really have a whole new system because your employer should be providing the basic system, we provide you with the add-ons'. But at that time it

was clear the health authority [her employer] were not going to provide; not going to budge. I think the process of applying for technical
support is a battle of wits. Employers bluff DAS by saying they won't
provide. DAS call the employers' bluff. Both sides wait to see if the applicant gives up the ghost; if they don't the whole thing starts again. You
have to be really persistent, especially where employers are in dispute
with DAS. It would have been so easy then just to carry on with the
typewriter. But I look back and think how intolerable the extra work
would be, having to type out similar letters.

(Mandy, secretary to social worker, blind;
attitude and environmental barriers)

While one can clearly see the fall-out from these negative attitudes, it is
more difficult to isolate the exact attitudes underlying these access problems.
What is more clear is that the voices of disabled people defining new technology needs, entering the planning, decision-making and provisory process,
would begin to challenge these negative attitudes.

The above access issues relate mainly to the acquisition of specialized technologies through specialist authorities. A wider and more commonly cited
result of attitude barriers was the limitation of access to technology already
in place. Here technology, chiefly of a mainstream type, was reported to be
difficult to access because of colleague and employer attitudes. What were
these attitudes?

Attitudes that limit enabling technology use

Ample evidence exists suggesting that the way technology is used – the limits
and cultural assumptions around its use – often excludes disabled workers,
workers who are not therefore able to get the full potential out of a given
technology. Such comments come from a range of workers, both technology
users and computer workers, and also from workers with a range of impairments facing a variety of barriers. The first example of limits to technology
use is of William, a former programmer. Here he refers to the way that his
employer's overall approach to business shaped his experiences:

The biggest problem was reading things, and also the occasional bad
quality of print – being tight-fisted they would always let the ribbon
run twice as long as they ought to. For me this was a real pain, even
though it would have cost the company pennies to buy a new printer
ribbon. My manager knew the difficulties I had as I had to use my hand
lens to read most things. The faint ribbon seemed to cancel out the real
benefit of computer-generated material – the ability to enlarge and play
about with text and images. What use is this if the printout is sub-
standard?

(William, unemployed programmer, visual impairment;
attitude, environmental and technical barriers)

It is difficult to determine the extent to which employers were aware of the result of their disabling working practices, and how conscious they were of the disabled worker's disadvantage. However, the barriers cited often seemed to be the result of employer and colleague ignorance rather than any active process. This conclusion might be drawn from the following transcripts reporting the limited use of e-mail, a communication aid that is seen by many disabled users as having obvious potential in providing communicative choice:

I think that e-mail could be useful, it's something I use to cut down on the amount of journeys I have to make, including less treks to the post room; but this system is hardly used as nobody else [able-bodied workers] likes it. Or so they say. I think this is a clear example of colleagues being wary of something new. It all seems a bit threatening. Someone at work hasn't read their e-mail for seven months. I know how valuable electronic mail is for me, but how do you educate colleagues to this. It would seem pushy for me to tell them; especially as I'm one of the youngest and newest members of staff. So, in an ideal world I would use e-mail even more.

(Gordon, finance officer, spina bifida, wheelchair user;
attitude and environmental barriers)

Similarly:

Some on the group do use it [e-mail], but people do not always answer. I would like to use it, but it takes two to communicate. E-mail might one day seem second nature like the phone, time will tell. I guess my need to use it is more urgent than with, say, hearing people. They will no doubt stick with the phone for quick messages, you haven't got the bother of signing in. Also e-mail is a bit like an answering machine, where you feel obliged to answer. With a phone, if you're not in you've none of these hang-ups. Obviously I'm one of those people who would rather not use the phone. But I'm against the grain as usual. So the issue is not whether e-mail is available, but whether people are motivated to use it. In that way it's only as effective as the number of people prepared to use it.

(Edward, administrative officer, hearing impairment;
attitude, environmental technical barriers)

William describes how a disabled worker had received technology when colleagues had not; this seemed to cause resentment, which seems to confirm that it is ignorance of the significance of new technology for disabled people which is the root of much resentment:

If I got anything different to my colleagues you got animosity because others worry that they might be missing something, this mixed with an intolerance of difference. I think the fact that most people are discreet about their disability [impairment] means colleagues do not always connect one-off provision of technology with disabled access. For example, I would use a hand lens to help me screen read, but I'd be discreet about it. Ironically, if I'd been much more upfront about my visual disability I think they might have connected the IT with this more readily.

(William, unemployed programmer, visual impairment;
attitude, environmental and technical barriers)

Having looked at the more immediate experiences of attitudes, we should be able to see that attitudes vary in terms of their degree of transparency. However, what they all have in common is an end result that serves (at worst) to exclude disabled people from technology-inclusive work, (at best) to reduce skilled IT workers' access to new technology. This assessment of attitudes as barriers is best concluded and summed up by reassessing the overall shape and impact of negative attitudes. The following represent the starkest examples of the way attitudes may continue to create barriers in the working lives of disabled people.

Prejudice revisited

A number of comments suggested that in addressing the potential of new technology for reducing barriers, the technology was not the problem. It was the attitudes that heavily shaped their use:

Personally, technology is not the problem. It is people. I can take the advantage of new technology, it is getting the opportunity to use it. But it is probably going to be denied to me.You ask whether technology will allow me to communicate my abilities. In order to communicate something like that I need a recipient. There is no recipient. Technology has not been allowed to give me that chance. I cannot begin to convey my frustration and anger about the way I've been treated. I feel like I'm hitting my head against a brick wall. I'm 46, I've tried for promotion to EO four times over a period of 15 years. I put that down to prejudice, pure and simple. Quite honestly feeling the way I do means my answers are probably not what you want to hear about the 'benefits' of computers. It's the human bit that's the biggest problem. The technology is there already, we can even put people on the moon. But getting to the moon would be easier than changing views about deafness. That's the real issue.

(Edward, administrative officer, hearing impairment;
attitude, environmental and technical barriers)

Edward seems to be saying the worst: new technology could redefine his abilities by allowing the expression of new skills previously denied by a disabling environment, but in order to show these new abilities he would need a willing recipient, something notably absent from his working life. Edward provides a valuable insight by arguing that when he applies for promotion he is seen as a deaf worker and, he feels by implication, an inferior worker. Although the quality and quantity of his work are, he thinks, as good as his colleagues, his supervisors fail to notice. As Edward put it, 'How else can you explain my failure to get even this modest promotion? My bosses simply refuse to accept that I can be deaf and be competent.' The fact that Edward could not gain EO status has meant that he has been unable to enter his preferred career area of programming, a form of work where having a hearing impairment is of little material significance to the completion of the work.

Other comments convey a similar message:

> I don't think that technology will equalize employment. Because people still have a stigma about disabled people. I don't think it will matter what you do, people will still see you as disabled, also I think a lot of employers aren't aware of the technology that could be used to employ disabled people.
>
> (Susan, purchasing officer, rheumatoid arthritis;
> attitude and environmental barriers)

One participant, a manager who took part in recruitment decisions, comments that attitudes have, if anything, hardened to reflect the austerity of the 1980s and 1990s:

> I think attitudes have hardened over the last few years in this organization. I don't think there is the understanding of 'tolerances' there was. One example is that we have just taken on 120 people this last year, and I don't think there are any disabled [*sic*]. I know the man in charge of the initial training programme, and recruitment policy has hardened. With the employment situation we can take the pick of the crop. As a disabled person myself, and someone who was given the opportunity to work and progress, I feel very bad about this. Sadly, wearing my manager's hat I have to say that the pressure is on to avoid recruiting what are seen to be employment risks and added costs. It's a bleak picture, but I hope it's not irreversible. Otherwise disabled managers will be a rare species by the time I retire.
>
> (Tony, computer services manager, visual impairment;
> environmental barriers)

The broader shift in economic and social policy augurs badly for disabled people as they are likely to face an increasingly hostile approach to recruitment and retention. However, the political dominance of free market economics in the 1980s and 1990s may in turn give way to a more propitious policy environment (see Chapter 11). We should not assume that this momentous shift in policy will be the last word on the subject; however, the hegemonic power of capitalism in the late twentieth century may ensure that parties of both left and right err on the side of market-driven policy rather than humanely inspired policy first and foremost.

Conclusion

Although in the previous chapter disabled people report the many benefits of new technology, continuing barriers suggest attitudes – ranging from minor and perhaps easily resolved barriers, to fundamental and ingrained attitude barriers – have to change fundamentally if the benefits of new technology are to be fully realized.

The final part of this work will attempt to begin a process of consolidation. Firstly, the quantitative and qualitative findings of this research will be drawn together to establish key developments in the enabling use of new technology, and the limits to that process. This will form the basis of substantial policy recommendations for more enabling experiences of working life.

 **PART 3**

CONCLUSIONS AND POLICY POINTS

 **10**

Conclusions

Having looked in some detail at the empirical findings of this research, it is now time to return to the key theoretical issues concerning the enabling potential of new technology, and the factors that continue to limit this process. The ensuing conclusions will then be used to reassess the value of a barriers approach in the study of new technology and disabled people. Attention will focus on the continued centrality of barriers in the working lives of disabled people, particularly the significance, resilience and power of attitude barriers.

Key findings

The findings indicate the obvious benefits of new technology in the lives of disabled workers and job seekers. The majority of participants felt that new technology had in some way begun to enhance their employment as disabled workers. This process of enhancement varied, from those who cited minor changes in their working practice which allowed more control of everyday work and workplace environments, through to workers who felt that they had been enabled in a more fundamental sense. In this sense disabled people felt that by using new technology they had been able to reappraise the disability–ability relationship, and begin to see themselves much more in terms of what they *were able to do*. For some, this enabling process reversed a lifelong conditioning which suggested that as a disabled person they were definable in terms of what they *could not do*. This near-unanimous citing of benefits, however, masks many negative experiences.

Of those researched, many felt that they were held back by continued barriers. Here, barriers included poor employment facilities, limited workplace access, inadequate training, underuse and misuse of new technology, and the continued presence of disabling attitudes. Two parallel points were clearly evident in the research findings. Firstly, the very barriers new technology has the potential to reduce long-term were continuing to limit the more immediate enabling use of new technology. That is, new technology is not immune from the disabling barriers it has the potential to attenuate. This has profound implications for the planned use of new technology in the enabling process.

Secondly, what was also clear from the study was that the use and experience of new technology was shaped by a set of interacting barriers; these were identified as 'configured' barriers. Consequently benefits and barriers have to be viewed 'in the round' if any progress is to be made in understanding disabled workers' experiences. For example, attitude, environmental and technical barriers in the lives of disabled people are configured and linked via historical, cultural, environmental and organizational assumptions about disability. The findings of this study also suggest the primacy of attitude barriers as the source of most other barriers, as the majority of remaining barriers can be linked at some point to attitudes more generally. The significance of the notion of 'configured' barriers is that a failure to recognize the linked nature of barriers could lead to the continuation of piecemeal, incremental approaches to overcoming barriers.

A number of other points of significance came out of the study. Firstly, that the beneficiaries of new technology did not conform to the 'state-of-the-art' image of high technology interventions that permeate deficit model analyses of technological benefits (Schofield 1981; Scherer and Galvin 1994; Hawkridge and Vincent 1985; Sandhu 1987; Chamot in Perlman and Hansen 1989: 10–14; for a rare critique see Cavalier in Gartner and Joe 1987). This focus can be seen as an ideological construction of the 'important' issues in disability and technology. In fact there was a spread of disabled beneficiaries in diverse employment situations, a range of technology use, varied forms of impairment and so on. Most disabled workers reported benefits stemming from relatively low technology devices. The equating of the benefits of new technology to dramatic interventions owes more to perceptions of high technology medicine than to the more appropriate focus on the more numerous, less 'scientific', less 'specialized' aids and devices (Karpf 1988: 149–61). Most benefits cited had been realized in the everyday arena of employment using mainstream technologies. The message from the research seems to be that if any further benefits are to flow from new technology in employment, it is primarily (but not solely) going to be in such settings.

A second important point, one related loosely to the previous point, is that most benefits reported were serendipitous rather than planned. Most disabled workers realized the benefits of new technology themselves and without the planned interventions of employers, personnel, rehabilitation workers or Employment Service staff. The implications for this research are that the role of the planned use of new technology, both mainstream and specialized, could be developed much further; but only where disabled people have a pivotal role in this planning.

More specific conclusions: configured benefits

The following analysis suggests that the triangulated data from the quantitative and qualitative stages of this research can be used to provide a fuller picture of those conditions under which configured benefits are most likely to be realized. Questionnaire findings showed that 90 per cent of respondents perceived benefits of new technology in enhancing both employee satisfaction and creating more enabling environments; however, those factors which allowed the fullest realization of benefits were not clear from any simple quantitative analysis. Here, interview material helped identify those participants most likely to report a number of benefits as high status, managerial or senior computer workers, working in large, public sector organizations with mild and moderate impairments (self-defined) which were not felt to be visible to managers and colleagues. In these instances employment that was senior enough to allow flexibility also meant that new technology could be used in a way that allowed maximum benefits in barrier reduction.

The ability to alter working patterns, and to manipulate physical and communication environments was significantly enhanced by seniority. Significantly, 'computer work' was synonymous with seniority for most disabled computer personnel. This was reflected in their equating of computer work (typically programming and systems analysis) with professional status. Computing seemed to allow more flexibility and self-directed barrier reduction than the generally lower status of 'technology use'. This had implications for the disabled women in the research as they were less likely to be in high status and computer work. Although a number of women had very positive experiences of enabling technology as senior programmers or managers, broadly the disabled women researched reported less enabling benefits of new technology in their work. This reflects women's under-representation in computer and managerial work. However, the continued dominance of men in computing, managerial and professional work may begin to explain why women are underrepresented. (On technology see Cockburn 1983, 1985; Harvey in Lee and Loveridge 1987: 72–82; Crompton and Sanderson 1990. On management see Witz 1992, and on the professions see Spencer and Podmore 1986; Spencer and Podmore in Lee and Loveridge 1987: 83–99.) There was no evidence, however, to suggest that women working in computing had less enabling experiences of new technology at work. Conversely, male technology users were in most instances as likely to cite the more modest impact of technology in the enabling process as were female technology users.

The dominance of men in computing is not simply numerical, but is reflected in the culture of computer work. Indeed, a number of women discussed their apprehension about the changes in their employment caused by new technology; this fear of technological change was not mentioned by disabled men. The assumed proximity of men to technology and their 'natural' connection with new technical devices can be described as a form of cultural capital that accrues more readily to men. This might be reinforced by the perception that men designed, installed and repaired new technologies. Again this cultural dominance was more evident in the more senior employment settings, where a number of disabled participants noted that they had been involved in the early development and use of microchip technologies.

One key factor enhancing the likelihood of configured benefits was the size of organization. The most enabling experiences were cited by employees working in large public sector organizations (usually over 100 employees). Conversely, small private organizations did not provide the same level of configured benefits generally. This does not suggest that small companies are inimical to an enabling environment, but that they appeared to be less likely on the whole to provide scope for configured benefits through new technology. Interview findings helped bring out these experiences. Here a number of participants referred to the 'knife-edge' nature of small business (see Bechhofer and Elliot 1981) and how business cycles heavily shaped the way technology was used; this often shaped disabled workers' experiences of how technology was used. In sum, small private organizations provided a less predictable set of work patterns, with technology use and barrier reduction even less likely to become a conscious organizational activity. It is worth remembering that self-employment was also cited by a number of participants as allowing enabling work. Again scope for greater autonomy was cited in this often self-directed form of work. However, the most enabling experiences were those cited by professionals working from home. Conversely, some of the least enabling experiences were cited by homeworkers who had insufficient work and who were highly dependent on scarce contract work. We should not claim therefore any inherent benefits of homeworking; we need to look at the specific nature of the homeworking arrangements. The key issue here is that for some workers, autonomy is enhanced by homeworking with new technology. For others, homeworking was a form of pseudo-employment, one which symbolized their marginal identity in employment terms (see Huws 1984; Allen and Wolkowitz 1987; Pennington and Westover 1989).

The question of the level of impairment of participants and reported benefits was significant, with the interview findings suggesting that severity of impairment altered perceived levels of benefits of new technology. Generally those participants experiencing least benefits were those with severe and clearly visible impairments (for example cerebral palsy). This finding suggests that the most pernicious attitudes reported limited those disabled people who might benefit most from a more enabling employment environment. A related point to come out of the interviews was that participants with severe impairments rejected the notion that pre-existing dependency relations may have influenced their ability to make use of new technology and employment opportunities. This casts doubt over the adequacy of theories of dependency which characterize much deficit model research on new technology (Croxen 1982). Indeed, participants detailed their efforts to struggle against dependency, which although often unsuccessful, suggests that Croxen's formulation of disabled people being ill-prepared for the responsibilities of computer work is inappropriate. Arguably, social model research has also been over-reliant on notions of dependency in the lives of disabled people, and while rightly encouraging collective struggle against dependency, such theories may have overlooked the role and significance of struggle in the everyday lives of disabled people (Barton 1989; Barnes 1991; Oliver 1990). Significantly, disabled people's collective struggle against disabling barriers may succeed most where it connects with previously isolated personal struggles.

In sum, for most workers the benefits of new technology were not unique to disabled people. These benefits were different, however, in the *degree* to which they enabled workers with impairments to gain access to the 'core text' of the employment environment. However, specialized technology did provide a minority of participants with what they identified as unique and particular benefits. What is significant is that although impairment is a key variable in shaping the experiences and perceptions of new technology, the basic relationship between the configured benefits of new technology and the impact on disabling environments is the same across the full range of personal experiences and forms of technology. The assertion that new technology is significant because of its potential to redefine disabling barriers is supported by users of both mainstream and specialized technologies. Here, the benefits of new technology are conspicuous by the absence of any objective alteration of an individual's impairment; this is a direct challenge to the medical model, which understands the benefits of new technology to consist of their ability to correct or augment bodily deficits (Sandhu 1987; MacFarlane 1990; Cornes in Oliver 1991: 98–114).

It was very clear that the fullest realization of the benefits of enabling technology is highly dependent upon a wider supportive and flexible environment. We can imagine this as a virtuous cycle of benefits. In the research the best examples of enabling technology were provided by disabled workers who felt that new technology had allowed a fundamental re-evaluation of their abilities and potential. Those abilities made possible by new technology produced an enhanced self-perception and an increasing awareness of the relationship between new technology, attitudes and the disabling process. Here is a simple model of this virtuous cycle:

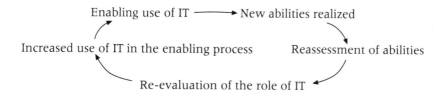

Notably, the cycle was only cited by two of the participants, and entailed re-evaluation by the disabled person only, and did not involve employers and co-workers in any conscious re-evaluation of disabled employees' abilities. Even these benefits were affected by continuing barriers. What were these barriers?

Continued barriers

Although 81 per cent of questionnaire respondents cited continued barriers in their work, this figure hides a range of enhanced experiences of barriers. The most compelling examples of continued barriers in the research relate to the continued weight of discriminatory attitudes. This finding suggests that negative constructions of disablement and difference continue to shape the experiences of disabled people (see Finkelstein 1980 for a seminal discussion of the power of disabling attitudes; and Barnes 1990: 77–80; Graham *et al.* 1990). Indeed, not only are attitude barriers the key factor in limiting the extent of the benefits of new technology, they also at some point create most other barriers. Thus environmental, technical and structural barriers can all be traced back at some point to discriminatory attitudes.

The continued impact of attitude barriers did not affect all participants similarly. Questionnaire and interview findings suggested that gender, employment status and the nature of impairment were important factors; high status, male workers with mild, moderate or hidden impairments were more insulated from these attitude barriers. However, this insulation was not total, and for the vast majority of disabled people such attitudes clearly tempered the potential benefits of new technology.

These negative attitudes affected the whole range of employment experiences, from the discrimination faced by disabled people trying to obtain new technology employment to the failure of skilled disabled workers to gain promotion; they also affected access to new technology and employer recognition of its benefits. The potential for a virtuous cycle of enabling technology was undermined by the attitudes of employers and colleagues. The failure or refusal of employers and colleagues to take note of the potential of new technology was a significant and lamentable feature of the remaining barriers disabled workers faced.

In two instances new technology was introduced and used in such a way that it actually led to the unemployment of the disabled participant. Here then is the antithesis of enabling technology, where employers and managers have failed to identify employment practices that combine economic with enabling imperatives.

Another example of disabling experiences surrounding the acquisition and use of new technology was that of the working of the Special Aids to Employment scheme (SAE). Although a number of workers successfully acquired new technology through the SAE, this success was overshadowed by the negative attitudes of the providers. More fundamentally, the scheme's assumptions about the nature of disablement meant that many disabled workers and job seekers were not assisted because they could not satisfy the physical eligibility requirements of the scheme, even though they felt they would be further enabled by such support. Questionnaire data indicated the dearth of specialized technology in use, and correspondingly, the small amount of technology provided through the SAE scheme. Interviews with disabled workers helped explain this small-scale provision in highlighting the narrow eligibility (or rationing) criteria adopted and the often unhelpful and opaque nature of the scheme's operation.

Non-disabled definitions of disability underlying the working of the scheme ensured that those applicants who were perceived to be 'too disabled' or 'not disabled enough' were not assisted. The SAE scheme operated firmly within the deficit model and was based upon the satisfaction of such physical eligibility criteria as conceived of by Employment Service staff. The scheme provided disabled people with little or no say in the nature or working of the scheme and seemed designed primarily to limit provision to 'special' technology and to employees with severe 'disabilities' [impairments]. The experiences of the SAE scheme suggest that its policy premises and operation are disabling, as no attempt is made to understand the enabling process, or to address the wider barriers in the workplace. Given this finding, any piecemeal revision of the SAE scheme is untenable. An enabling new technology scheme for disabled workers and job seekers would have to prioritize the views of disabled people themselves and ask the fundamental questions: what is enabling about new technology? what other factors contribute to this enabling process? and how can an equitable and enabling technology access scheme be formulated? This would include a reassessment of the role and benefits of new technology in the lives of disabled workers, and the function of new technology in redefining notions of disability and ability. Such a scheme would turn the focus of attention increasingly upon the employment and para-employment barriers disabled people face.

Recent developments

The government's persistent attempts to make employers contribute towards the costs of special employment measures for disabled workers (*Disability Now* 1993, 1995b: 4; Beinart *et al.* 1996) can only be seen as a retrograde step in the light of the above findings. Here the advent of the Access to Work Scheme (ATW), and a request for an employers' contribution to all 'disability-related' costs for workers who have been employed for at least six months, risk creating even further barriers to disabled workers (Scott-Parker in *Disability Now* 1993: 9). At a general level employers may be even less likely to employ disabled workers, and less likely to keep them on for more than six months. The most worrying aspect of the changes mooted with the ATW scheme is its shift towards a means-tested scheme, with increasingly disabling eligibility tests. Although evidence suggests that ATW budgets have risen significantly since its introduction in 1994, a parallel shift towards targeting the scheme means that existing employees not in receipt of ATW support are unable to claim special aids and employment support (Shephard cited in *Disability Now* 1996a: 14). Evidence has also come to light of refusals to fund additional support to existing beneficiaries (*Disability Now* 1995b: 1–2).

While the decision to make employers contribute to the provision of new technology might appear a positive step – perhaps the first attempt to encourage employers to recognize workplace barriers – no evidence exists to suggest that employers are more ready to view new technology as an enabling tool for disabled people. The result of this policy shift may simply be a shift towards buck passing in the field of technology provision (on the growth of such 'pillar to post' welfarism see Walker in Bornat *et al.* 1993).

Despite much evidence of continued barriers, there might be some grounds for optimism about the future of enabling technology use. Firstly, with the increased ubiquity of desktop technology (Gill 1985; Daniel 1987; Lane in Gallie 1988: 68–73; Kling and Ianoco in Forester 1989: 336–7), the scope for a wholesale realization of the benefits of new technology for disabled people may increase. This may also be assisted by the reduction in the costs of new technology over the next 20 years. This cost reduction should help make new technology even more commonplace in the workplace. The spread of new technology into education, training and rehabilitation will also increase disabled people's access to new technology. Educational mainstreaming can only be a positive development in this respect (see Barton 1988; Booth *et al.* 1992). However, these positive developments cannot be divorced from the resilience of attitude barriers. The following attempts to round off the issues of concern in any process of furthering enabling technology use.

A barriers approach: redefining the role of technology

An important theoretical and methodological task of this study was the examination of the validity and strength of a barriers approach in the study of new technology and employment experiences. It was argued at the outset that a deficit model had dominated thinking about the role of new technology, according to which the positive role of new technology lay in the correction of or compensation for a person's impairment. The research, in exploring the exact functions of new technology, has discovered that the enabling process has *not* changed the impairment objectively, and that the real function of new technology lies in its potential to reduce the wider barriers faced by disabled workers. The findings suggest that a barriers focus is the most valuable for understanding the actual relationship between technology and disablement. Indeed, the key (but not exclusive) axis of concern is not that of new technology and impairment, but of new technology and disablement. The latter can be equated with the attitudes, ideological structures and physical obstacles which together form the barriers investigated in this study.

Conclusion

The above findings provide a comprehensive picture of the role of new technology in the working lives of disabled people. The results highlight the ways in which new technology is beneficial for disabled people in redefining their workplace and, in a few instances, in changing attitudes to workers with impairments. The above analysis also provides a comprehensive picture of the barriers that still remain in the contemporary workplace. However, evidence suggests that some disabled people were substantially more likely to face continued barriers because of their pre-existing employment status. The research provides a number of clues as to how disabled people could best secure the enabling potential of new technology in their employment. A small number of research findings point to new technology use being a detrimental experience, and reasons for this are explored.

The above findings strongly support the value of a social barriers model in evincing the role and dynamics of enabling and disabling employment structures. In redefining the research 'problem' away from impairment to disablement, from individual physical deficits to organizational and social barriers, the study has advanced our understanding of the enabling/disabling workplace. Clearly this proven value of a barriers approach has applicability to disability research more generally. The research suggested that a barriers approach fits well with qualitative methods where the subtleties of barriers and ideological constructions of disablement can be explored. However, the value of quantitative background material was also established where it was supported by triangulated experience-based qualitative material.

The implications, then, of barriers research for any policy planning is clear. The focus of policy has to shift to those wider social barriers that are shaping (facilitating or limiting) workers' experiences of new technology. This involves a parallel shift away from the individual as the 'problem' in social policy. It is to the policy implications of this research that we now turn.

 **11**

Enabling technology policy and social rights

In line with the objective that this research directly contributes to the lives of disabled people, that ideas inform practice, the findings of this study will be translated where possible into policy recommendations – specific proposed institutions or legislation is identified in italics. This chapter also identifies the need to place technology policy into a rights-based framework in a way that challenges previously 'needs'-based policies and practices. Such a policy analysis can usefully be broken down into the following:

- general policy environment;
- pre- and para-employment measures;
- employment and new technology policy.

Enabling technology and the general policy environment

Given that specific enabling policies are not likely to prosper in a wider social environment which is disabling, it is important to position particular policy recommendations within a more general policy framework (Stubbins 1987: 59–64; Niwa 1988: 119). A useful way of discerning the most appropriate policy environment is to make cross-national comparisons. If we were asked to identify two countries in which a rights-based policy discourse has gained most currency we could cite the United States and Sweden. At first glance two more diverse countries would be hard to find, at least in policy terms. However, both equate closely, although imperfectly, to a rights-based policy structure.

In what ways do Sweden and the United States create what can be described as a rights-based policy framework? Sweden has by general consensus created perhaps the most generous work and welfare programmes of the advanced industrial economies (Esping-Andersen 1990; Ginsburg in Cochrane and Clarke 1993: 173–203), and although facing the same harsh economic realities as the rest of Europe, the Swedish state's commitment to full employment and social equality remains intact. The social rights given to workers and welfare claimants stem from a corporatist compact between state, employers and worker representatives. In exchange for this compact, the state has attempted to maximize employment, with generous support for formerly excluded people (Active Manpower Policy). In this way Sweden has administered a successful programme of rehabilitation, training, special aids provision and sheltered employment schemes (Swedish Handicap Institute 1981, 1992: 20–1) while also encouraging designers, universities, employers and the Swedish disability movement to work together in developing a technology assistance policy and specific initiatives such as the Technology Procurement for Persons with Disabilities in Vocational Life, or TUFFA project (see Breding in British Computer Society 1990: 70–3).

While Sweden is a useful model for enabling employment and technology policy, the heavy reliance on the role of the state in disability rights is not likely to be well received by some disability commentators who emphasize the importance of the individual in policy terms. This may augur badly for a neo-corporatist approach being adopted in the United Kingdom. (For a right-wing commentary on the primacy of the individual over statutory interventions see the work of Frank Bowe 1978, 1980; for a left-wing discussion of the role of disabled people's self-organization as a corrective to state activity see Shakespeare 1993: 249–64.)

What can be called a 'corporatist social rights' approach in Sweden can be contrasted with what might be dubbed the 'legal rights' approach of the United States. Here the growth of broad legislative rights can be seen to offer legal redress for discrimination against disabled people. The 1973 Rehabilitation Act and the 1990 Americans with Disabilities Act provide discrete but complementary rights; they provide for both proactive rights and reactive law suits after discrimination has occurred. Proactive legal rights take the form of affirmative employment policies (Sections 501 and 503 of the 1973 Act) where federal employers and contractors to federal agencies are asked to identify barriers to disabled people's employment, and to construct plans detailing how they are going to reduce these barriers, and the timescale of these changes (Gooding 1994: 86). Other examples of proactive law are the 1980 Telecommunications Accessibility Enhancement Act (Edwards in British Computer Society 1990: 22; Gooding 1994: 91) which requires federal employers to make telecommunications equipment accessible to all employees. In practical terms this means that employees with a hearing impairment should be provided with the equivalent telecommunication equipment such as a text phone. Additionally, the 1986 amendment to the 1974 Rehabilitation Act requires that computer designers and suppliers who sell to federal authorities should build access features into the design of computer hardware and software (see Edwards in British Computer Society 1990: 23).

The Americans with Disabilities Act (1990) represents the apotheosis of a legal rights approach; however, as the analysis of the Act below suggests, the reliance on abstract legal rights not only places disabled people firmly within the domain of lawyers, it also represents a fiercely individualist interpretation of rights based on formal principles of law with no guaranteed outcomes. The passing of Britain's first anti-discrimination statute for disabled people in the 1995 Disability Discrimination Act illustrates the British government's preference for an individual and (dilute) legal approach to social rights in the United Kingdom.

While the proactive aspects of American law are promising for disabled workers, and notwithstanding the scope for 'class actions' in American law (Gooding 1994: 102), the reliance on individualized legal responses after discrimination has occurred represents a problem for disabled people. This individualized approach to social rights via legal process contrasts strongly with the Swedish corporatist approach of trying to build enabling structures into employment and training. The latter has to be seen as preferable to the extent that it tries to avoid acrimonious case law by corporate planning of disability services and provision. This does not rule out the possible role of such remedial-style laws supplementing Swedish social policy at some future point, but the present system privileges the power of collective over individual remedies, proactive planning over reactive justice. Although the state retains a key role in the Swedish model of social rights, it alone can combine planned access to employment and new technology with issues of social equity.

Although having distinct policy imperatives, and diverse interpretations of what social rights mean and how they are delivered, the American and Swedish experiences both represent positive examples of more enabling policy structures; and they are not inherently exclusive of each other. Not only have these countries gone much further in attempting to apply enabling Acts, but both can also lay claim to very active disability movements. (On Sweden see Driedger 1989: 31; Swedish Handicap Institute/Keijer 1992: 20; on the disability movement in the United States see Driedger 1989: 21–3; Gooding 1994: 20–2.)

A key challenge in providing a suitable policy environment is the dovetailing of statutory measures (whether corporatist or legalist) with a commitment to involve disability movements and the voices of disabled people in the construction, review and amendment of disability policy (Zarb in Oliver 1991: 178–203; Beresford and Harding 1993; Shakespeare 1993; Stephenson and Parsloe 1993; Barnes 1997: 46–71).

New technology and a new policy agenda: a rights approach

The following analysis should begin to clarify why anti-discrimination legislation and a rights-based discourse is a necessary but insufficient prerequisite of enabling technology policy and provision. A barriers approach to the role of new technology identifies its potential to reduce the social and environmental barriers to disabled people's achievements. How does this same approach view the basic policy issues at stake? Instead of discussing 'needs', this approach sees the importance of *rights* in an enabling technology provision. Access to new technology is here viewed as a right for all those disabled people who could use it to reduce the barriers they themselves identify in their working lives. The notion of rights should not simply relate to rights of access to new technology, but to the non-disabling design, delivery, facilitation and back-up of new technology.

A needs-based policy should be rejected because it is essentially negative, stating that recipients have to be physically different, lacking or 'needy' to qualify for help. A policy based on rights is inherently positive: it rejects the need for disabling eligibility tests, and is concerned with the barriers faced by disabled people.

The language of 'needs' fostered such terms as 'compensatory technology', and 'special aids'. A new approach based upon rights would identify with such terms as 'joint access planning', 'access audits', 'environmental access order' and 'workplace rehabilitation'. The particular circumstances of a disabled worker need not be overlooked in this equation. However, the beginning, middle and end of rights-based new technology policy would be the barriers and rehabilitation of the broader working environment. Here one can see how the twin stimuli of anti-discrimination legislation and more-specific technology access policies need to be dovetailed to provide enhanced physical and attitude environments. The idea that anti-discrimination legislation would be enough by itself to secure enabling policies is highly questionable.

Why anti-discrimination legislation is not enough

The Americans with Disabilities Act (ADA) 1990 and the UK Disability Discrimination Act (DDA) 1995 are too recent to allow definitive judgements as to their success, but early commentaries suggest that anti-discrimination legislation will only operate with clear developments around the process and definition of discrimination (Barnes 1990b; Edwards in British Computer Society 1990: 24; *Equal Opportunities Review* 1990: 28–9; Graham *et al.* 1990: 17; Bradshaw 1991: 17–18; Bynoe *et al.* 1991; Gooding 1994).

As the ADA has had more time to take effect we will concentrate on the efficacy and limits of that statute, and as the DDA embodies many of the legal principles of the ADA we can predict the likely weaknesses of the DDA from the American experience. The ADA itself states that discrimination against a 'qualified person' is illegal, and that 'reasonable accommodations' should be made to the workplace to allow equal access. Here, a 'qualified person' is one who can perform the 'essential functions' of a job, but given the complex nature of new technology benefits we can easily see how discrimination could operate, both consciously and inadvertently in the absence of a parallel technology policy. For example, many workers could not do essential functions of a job without a range of technologies, that is, technology not 'ordinarily used' (by able-bodied workers) in a given job. Is this outside of the 'essential function' test? Would such technology be viewed as a reasonable accommodation?

The ADA lays down guidelines for the operation of the 'reasonable accommodation' clause, which states that such accommodations should be made where it would not impose 'undue hardship'. One can clearly see how 'the essential functions', 'reasonable accommodations' and 'undue hardship' clauses may be used to avoid the employment of disabled people, especially where it would involve technology provision. This suggests that to have anti-discrimination legislation without parallel access legislation may allow new technology to be overlooked in the enabling process (see Massie 1994). It is worth stating at this point that while the American reliance on civil rights-based legislation is positive, the economic and ideological climate that shapes American public and economic policy may prove inimical to enabling technology provision, one where the market not the state is seen to hold most of the answers to employment and technological questions. Conversely, the United Kingdom (with no history of constitutional civil rights) has placed more emphasis on the role of state intervention between the individual and the market, and in welfare provision (see Bowe 1980; Friedmann *et al.* 1987: 1–44 and 83–110).

The advantages of introducing anti-discrimination legislation into a country that has a history of commitment to state intervention in employment and welfare is clear. However, even the most thoroughgoing legislative programme would not be enough by itself to guarantee the enabling use of new technology. Here the history of the workings of the Sex Discrimination Act (West 1982: 150–3) and Race Relations Acts (Lustgarten and Edwards in Braham *et al.* 1992: 270–93) suggests that legislation is not a panacea, and that these laws are often operated in sexist and racist terms. Success within the terms of equal opportunities laws is commonly a pyrrhic victory, given the efforts involved in resorting to law and the often derisory outcomes of legal tribunals. The added fact that new technology is not viewed in terms of rights in the same way as access to employment and equal pay suggests that wider measures will have to be taken to ensure the enabling process is furthered. What are these wider measures?

One key way in which anti-discrimination legislation could be improved is to build disabled people into the process of appraising what is/is not a 'reasonable accommodation'. For too long non-disabled people generally, and (in the employment domain) employers and statutory bodies, have been the arbiters of reasonable practice.

The issue then is not that of the redundancy of the term 'reasonable accommodation' as practical issues of the size and solvency of an organization and the finite statutory funds for access are important, but the power of those who decide on these reasonableness criteria. We can begin to look at how this monopoly of decision-making can be changed.

Designing disabled people in

In order that the design and functioning of personal computers fit with the requirements of workers with a variety of impairments, the notion of a voice for disabled people is particularly important. The design stage has been undervalued as an arena in which barriers can be reduced at source; barriers that relate to the basic technologies themselves. This process is not likely to be easy because the values and attitudes of designers themselves can serve as a major barrier to such a voice: 'Unfortunately, we cannot simply talk to [disabled] people and ask them what they need, these products are not like motor cars or washing machines, because the customers themselves may not be the best judges of what they need' (Wolff in Brechin *et al.* 1981: 46).

The message of this book is that disabled technology users *are* best placed to know what they need to gain greater access to their working environment. To ignore this is a gross undervaluation of the potential role disabled people could have in shaping new technology at the design stage. America again has seen most attempts to cater for the requirements of disabled people. This has generally involved decisions where disabled people are represented by 'experts' in the field of new technology and disability. These are often disabled academics, computer designers and rehabilitation workers. While this is not the same as an inclusion of disabled people generally, it is a step in that direction. One major factor that has led to this involvement has been the implementation of design legislation under Section 508 of the Rehabilitation Act (1973, amended 1986).

This measure aims to build accessibility into all new technology, so that disabled people have maximum inclusion in using these products. Unfortunately the provisions only apply to equipment supplied to US federal agencies. A similar piece of legislation again only applying to the federal arena is the Telecommunications Accessibility Enhancement Act (TAEA). As mentioned earlier, this Act specifies minimum accessibility specifications for telecommunications equipment. These two pieces of legislation are not presented as *the model* of designing disabled people in, indeed the federal remit of the schemes means they are self-limiting (see Mendelsohn in Perlman and Hansen 1989: 28; Edwards in British Computer Society 1990: 26). What is important about these Acts is that they illustrate the possible way forward, one where design, accessibility criteria and consumer involvement all have a central part to play in making new technology effective as an enabling force.

Alongside design legislation modelled on these US Acts, in the UK a *National Access Design Council* would bring together the state, university engineering departments (UMIST at Manchester and CREST at Newcastle are likely players in this regard), enlightened rehabilitation workers and, importantly, radical disability organizations. This joint approach is very much modelled on the Swedish Handicap Institute and its satellite projects (for example the Swedish National Board for Industrial and Technical Development). Much emphasis would be given to avoiding the dominance of a technicist approach characteristic of the EU's TIDE (Technology Initiative for Disabled and Elderly People) Programme. Significantly, the politics of new technology provision should be viewed as central to an enabling future for disabled workers. Technical, design and ergonomic issues would begin to be viewed as an adjunct of the enabling process, not the defining principle.

Access legislation

In order to make access a meaningful idea and not simply a slogan devoid of any real significance, access has to be guaranteed, both to the immediate working environment through new technology, and to the wider environment. Tighter controls on the specifications of building regulations and the full use of broad anti-discrimination legislation measures would ensure greater access to jobs. As regards access within the workplace, the provisions for grant-aided environmental improvements embodied in the 1944 Employment Act (Disabled Persons) would be superseded by an *Access to Environments Act* (AEA). The operation of the AEA would be employee-led, would be overseen by a *Works Access Council* and would end the previous reliance on the employer's casting vote in the choice to adopt or reject building alterations. The success of the AEA would be underwritten by anti-discrimination measures which would make unwarranted refusals to alter workplace environments an offence.

In the arena of transport, tougher sanctions are needed to ensure major public and licensed operators commit themselves to accessible vehicles. One way in which such processes could be enhanced is via *joint access groups*. Here access to transport, leisure and employment would all be addressed (as configured barriers). Access groups would be made up of 18 access officers (in a city council of 250,000 to 2,000,000 inhabitants) and would consist of a two-thirds representation of elected disabled people, and a one-third representation of locally elected officers to include employers, transport operators, planners and local authority officials. Here the particular value of having anti-discrimination legislation as a buttress for deciding access rights would mean that these groups would have a statutory duty to provide accessible environments. The decisions of a joint access group would be binding under the joint statutory measures of anti-discrimination legislation and access laws.

In trying to establish positive measures for disabled people the establishment of a *National Access Coordination Group* (NACG) could allow for the design, monitoring, improvement and overall running of the scheme. The NACG would have to work in close collaboration with academics and disability groups who offered advice on questions as diverse as lessons from abroad (Sweden, and the United States for example), the changing preferences of disabled people, and major problems with access under the revised legislation.

The above general measures of anti-discrimination and access legislation, and the local access groups designed to ensure general access is achieved, will be the basic framework upon which more specific and focused policy measures will be made. Without this general framework it is likely that more-focused technology and employment policies will fail. Such legislation not only places a statutory duty on authorities towards equality and access measures, but equally as important, creates a climate of thought which suggests that the issue of disablement and access barriers is now firmly centre stage. Attention will now shift to these specific policies.

Pre-employment and para-employment policy and new technology

Pre-employment policy

The research findings suggested that barriers to new technology use were evident in educational, training, rehabilitation and assessment settings. One key factor limiting the enabling use of new technology appeared to be the ignorance of the potential of new technology. Here a *Disability and IT Awareness* campaign could begin to raise awareness levels among teachers, trainers, rehabilitation and assessment staff. The campaign would be coordinated by an *IT Awareness Task Force* made up of disabled people, disabled academics, computer company consortia and appropriate allies from education, rehabilitation and employment assessment spheres.

Higher education is a key area which can bridge education and employment in order to enhance employment opportunities with new technology. The present Disabled Students' Allowance funding for 'specialist equipment' goes some way to recognizing the role of new technology. But this is framed largely in terms of educational equipment or in terms of general access (ramps for example). One major advance would be for central Department for Education and Employment funding of any new technology device which enhances a disabled student's broader vocational opportunities. A *Vocational Aid through IT Scheme* would be funded centrally, given the capricious nature of local authority funding of 'discretionary' applications.

Staying within the realms of higher education, the recognition in the research that computer work was viewed as a highly satisfactory and suitable employment for many disabled participants suggests that an initiative to encourage disabled students into computing may be a worthwhile one. The increasing competition in the labour market for programming and analysis work also suggests that disabled people may have to use the increasingly recognized graduate route to enter such work. Here the funding of an initiative to enhance the numbers of disabled people on computing courses in higher education is a useful starting point. The Department for Education and Employment has a clear responsibility in the provision of funding for these purposes. Such a *Disabled People into Computing* initiative would send the right signals both to disabled people and would-be employers.

At-home technology

A major problem was identified by those disabled people who were unable to obtain employment but who felt that familiarization with new technology would give them a greater chance of getting work in the future. All of those suggesting that such at-home provision would be useful had some experience of new technology. In this case new technology had been seen as a potential boon but was proving almost impossible to acquire in the absence of work. These disabled people referred to a Catch-22 where they were unable to get work without the new technology, but were unable to get the new technology without the work. One obvious measure here could be for the loan of new technology to be extended to those who had been on and completed a recognized new technology course, but who could not find employment. Having access to new technology at home would allow the processes of familiarization and preparation for work to continue, especially where supported by ongoing vocational training.

An *IT and Disability Home Loan Scheme* be established for those disabled people wishing to continue to develop their new technology skills outside of work, but in preparation for it. Clearly the length of such a scheme would have to be set at, say, two years, and the end of the scheme followed up by the offer of further vocational support. Withdrawal of new technology should be handled cautiously and with an offer of continuity where it is realistic and preferred. Let us now turn to the central focus of this chapter, the question of employment and technology policy in enhancing the experiences of disabled people in late capitalism.

Employment and new technology policy

Access to Technology (ACT) legislation would mandate the government, specifically the Department for Education and Employment, to provide access to technology where it was felt that it would allow access to employment, an area of employment or promotion. Such technology and its support staff would be funded out of a grant/levy scheme via legislative backing as per the German, Swedish and Dutch models. (See the following: on Germany, Graham *et al.* 1990: 13; Barnes 1991: 95; Daunt 1992; Rowat 1992: 12. On Sweden see Carlsson and Carlsson 1982: 41; Breding 1991: 70. On the Netherlands see Croxen 1982: 32; and Barnes 1991.) This would allow predictable rates of funding for such technological support. An *Access to Technology Act* and an accompanying *Access to Technology Scheme* would allow rights to both mainstream and specialized technology, and would be provided to the disabled person, not the employer. This scheme would allow technological transferability. Its administration would involve a locally based (that is sub-regional) joint committee made up of one-third Employment Department representatives and employers themselves, one-third members of the local access group mentioned above, and one-third disabled people who are elected to represent all disabled workers. The idea of having disabled employee representatives again comes from Sweden, and helps formalize issues of access in the employment domain more generally. What any legislative scheme has to avoid is the squeezing of disabled applicants for technology by intransigent Employment Department staff and employers.

Challenging statutory technology policies?

A major set of conclusions in the research relate to the immediate shortcomings and disabling premises of the Special Aids to Employment scheme and its successor embodied in the Access to Work programme. Not only are these schemes disabling in the deficit model they adopt, but they are fraught with labyrinthine regulations and strict eligibility criteria. Their cash-limited nature, the absence of a ring fencing of funds, and their low status and priority all contribute to patchy and at times degrading schemes. The loser has clearly been the disabled applicant. One way to clarify the need for a new form of provision has been to ask: what can be learnt from the disabling premises and operation of these schemes?

It is in response to these questions that the above tenets of a new system were formulated. A rights-based, levy-financed system backed up by anti-discrimination legislation suggest themselves as the only way forward. The fundamental problem with the SAE scheme was its core disabling premises. Here no amount of fine tuning or increased funding (an administrative or revisionist approach: see Finkelstein in Oliver 1991: 19–39) could compensate. Correspondingly, Employment Service involvement in a revised scheme would risk diluting the benefits of a new Access to Technology Act and scheme. Only by completely overhauling the way new technology and disablement are framed theoretically can the cultural boundaries of the SAE scheme be undermined and redrawn. The above ideas do not discount completely the value of SAE and ATW staff, and their contribution to an Access to Technology scheme; however, the scheme risks failure unless those who wish to be involved enter a period of extensive retraining towards a rights-based scheme.

A number of subsidiary policy points need to be made regarding homeworking and self-employment – they both featured in the research itself as potentially beneficial areas of work with IT. Given the benefits of flexible work embodied in homeworking and the significance of self-employment for some disabled technology users, access legislation would have to extend its remit to encompass these groups. This would also discourage employers seeking loopholes around access legislation by marginalizing disabled employees into what are perceived to be less-protected working environments.

Concluding remarks

The above legislative and regulatory changes are only likely to be successful where broader social movements representing disabled people are evident. The history of the experiences of disabled people, and of the relationship between policy and change, suggests that it is only when such movements form the backdrop of national policy decisions that actual change occurs (see Carlsson and Carlsson 1982; Driedger 1989 and Oliver 1990: 123–31). While this book has not been concerned directly with the role and potential of social movements, its attempt to develop an emancipatory theoretical model and research methodology has to refer to Oliver's notion of 'counter-hegemonic' politics. Policy analysis, and the likelihood of it being acted upon by powerful social groups, relies on both the workability of a given set of policies and the belief that a groundswell of public opinion will eventually lead to intense pressure towards that policy. The success of these policies depends not simply on the efficient dissemination of these research recommendations, but more broadly on disabled people's readiness to take part in the promotion of these ideas. It is hoped that both research and disabled people's wider struggle can be mutually beneficial in any project to install a barriers consciousness into wider society.

References

Abberley, P. (1987) The concept of oppression and the development of a social theory of disability, *Disability, Handicap and Society*, 2(1): 5–19.

Albrecht, G. (1981) *Cross-National Rehabilitation Policies: A Sociological Perspective.* London: Sage.

Allen, S. and Wolkowitz, C. (1987) *Homeworking: Myths and Realities.* Basingstoke: Macmillan.

Ashley, J. (1974) *Journey into Silence.* London: Bodley Head.

Ashok, H., Hall, J. and Huws, U. (1985) *Home Sweet Workstation: Homeworking and the Employment Needs of People with Severe Disabilities.* London: Equal Opportunities Group, GLC.

Ashton, D. and Maguire, M.J. (1986) *Young Adults in the Labour Market.* Department of Employment Research Paper No. 55. London: HMSO.

Barker, J. and Downing, H. (1980) Word processing and the transformation of patriarchal relations in the office, *Capital and Class*, 10: 64–99.

Barker, R. (1990) I.T. for disabled people as an aid to life or a living. Conference paper, British Computer Society Disability Programme, November.

Barnes, C. (1990) *Cabbage Syndrome: The Social Construction of Dependence.* London: Falmer Press.

Barnes, C. (1991) *Disabled People in Britain and Discrimination: A Case for Anti-Discrimination Legislation.* London: Hurst and Co.

Barnes, M. (1997) *Care, Communities and Citizens.* London: Longman.

Barton, L. (ed.) (1988) *The Politics of Special Educational Needs.* London: Falmer.

Barton, L. (ed.) (1989) *Disability and Dependency.* London: Falmer.

Barton, L. (ed.) (1996) *Disability and Society: Emerging Issues and Insights.* London: Longman.

Barton, L. and Tomlinson, S. (eds) (1981) *Special Education: Policy, Practices and Social Issues.* London: Harper and Row.

Bechhofer, F. and Elliott, B. (eds) (1981) *The Petite Bourgeoisie: A Comparative Study of the Uneasy Stratum.* London: Macmillan.

Beinart, S., Smith, P. and Sproston, K. (1996) *The Access to Work Programme: A Survey of Recipients, Employers, Employment Service Managers and Staff.* London: Social and Community Planning Research.

Bell, D. (1974) *The Coming of Post Industrial Society. A Venture in Social Forecasting.* London: Heinemann.

Bell, D. (1980) The social transformation of the information society, in T. Forester (ed.) *The Microelectronics Revolution.* Oxford: Blackwell.

Beresford, P. and Harding, T. (eds) (1993) *A Challenge to Care: Practical Experiences of Building User-Led Services.* London: National Institute of Social Work.

Beveridge, W. (1942) *Social Insurance and Allied Services.* London: HMSO.

Blaxter, M. (1976) *The Meaning of Disability.* London: Heinemann.

Booth, T. and Swann, W. (1987) *Including Pupils with Disabilities.* Milton Keynes: Open University Press.

Booth, T., Swann, W., Masterton, M. and Potts, P. (eds) (1992) *Policies for Diversity in Education.* London: Routledge.

Bornat, J., Pereira, C., Pilgrim, D. and Williams, F. (eds) (1993) *Community Care: A Reader.* Basingstoke: Macmillan/Open University.

Borsay, A. (1986) Personal trouble or public issue? Toward a model of policy for people with mental and physical disabilities, *Disability, Handicap and Society,* 1(2): 179–97.

Bowe, F. (1978) *Handicapping America: Barriers to Disabled People.* New York: Harper and Row.

Bowe, F. (1980) *Rehabilitating America: Toward Independence for Disabled and Elderly People.* New York: Harper and Row.

Bradshaw, S. (1991) Citizenship rights, disabled people and anti-discrimination legislation, in *Contact,* Autumn. London: RADAR.

Braham, P., Rattansi, A. and Skellington, R. (eds) (1992) *Racism and Antiracism.* London: Sage.

Brechin, A., Liddiard, P. and Swain, J. (eds) (1981) *Handicap in a Social World.* Sevenoaks: Hodder and Stoughton/Open University.

Breding, J. (1991) The Tuffa project: technology for disabled people in working life, British Computer Society Sixth Annual Conference proceedings:'Europe, Markets and Politics'. London: British Computer Society.

Brisenden, S. (1987) A response to 'Disability in 1986 and Beyond': a report to the Royal College of Physicians, *Disability, Handicap and Society,* 2(2): 175–82.

British Computer Society (1990) Proceedings of the Sixth Annual Conference: 'Europe, Markets and Politics'. Warwick: British Computer Society Disability Programme.

Brown, C. (1984) *Black and White Britain.* London: Policy Studies Institute/Gower.

Brown, C. and Gay, P. (1985) *Racial Discrimination 17 years after the Act.* London: Policy Studies Institute.

Brown, P. and Scase, R. (eds) (1991) *Poor Work: Disadvantage and the Division of Labour.* Buckingham: Open University Press.

Busby, G. (1990) Technology support, *Journal of the British Computer Society's Disabled People and I.T. Support Group,* 7: 1.

Bynoe, I., Oliver, M. and Barnes, C. (1991) *Equal Rights for Disabled People: The Case for a New Law.* London: Institute for Public Policy Research.

Carew, J. and West, R. (1989) *Career Development for Visually Handicapped People Using I.T.* Report by the Central Communications and Telecommunications Agency. Report No. 38. Peterborough: CCTA.

Carlsson, B. and Carlsson, F. (1982) *Social Welfare and Handicap Policy in Sweden.* Stockholm: Swedish Handicap Institute.

Carver, V. and Rodda, M. (1978) *Disability and the Environment.* London: Paul Elek.

Church, C. and Glennen, S. (1992) *Handbook of Assistive Technologies.* Blackwell: Oxford.

Clare-Wenger, G. (1987) *The Research Relationship*. London: Allen and Unwin.

Clark, A. and Hirst, M. (1989) Disability in adulthood: a ten year follow-up of young disabled people, *Disability, Handicap and Society*, 4(3): 271–86.

Clarke, J., Cochrane, A. and McLaughlin, E. (eds) (1994) *Managing Social Policy*. London: Sage.

Cochrane, A. and Clarke, J. (eds) (1993) *Comparing Welfare States: Britain in an International Context*. London: Sage.

Cockburn, C. (1983) *Brothers: Male Dominance and Technological Change*. London: Pluto.

Cockburn, C. (1985) *Machinery of Dominance: Women, Men and Technical Knowledge*. London: Pluto.

Confederation of Indian Organizations (1987) *Double Bind: To be Disabled and Asian*. London: CIO.

CORAD (1982) *Report of the Committee on the Restrictions Against Disabled People*. London: HMSO.

Cornes, P. (1984) *The Future of Work for People with Disabilities: A View from Great Britain*. World Rehabilitation Fund Monograph No. 28. New York: WRF.

Cornes, P. (1987) *Impact of New Technology on the Employment of Persons with Disabilities in Great Britain*. Rehabilitation International/CEC. Brussels: Commission of the European Communities.

Cornes, P. (1989) *Effects of New Technology on the Employment of Disabled People with Severe Sensory or Physical Disabilities: Selected Case Studies from Ireland, Scotland and Sweden*. Paris: Organization for Economic Cooperation and Development.

Cornes, P. (1990) *New Technology Training Programmes for People with Disabilities in Great Britain*. New York: Rehabilitation International.

Crompton, R. and Sanderson, K. (1990) *Gendered Jobs and Social Change*. London: Unwin Hyman.

Croxen, M. (1982) *Disability and Employment*. Brussels: Commission of the European Communities.

Daniel, W.W. (1987) *Workplace Industrial Relations and Technical Change*. London: Frances Pinter.

Daunt, P. (1992) *Meeting Disability: A European Response*. London: Cassell.

Deegan, M. and Brooks, M. (eds) (1985) *Women and Disability: The Double Handicap*. New Brunswick, NJ: Transaction Books.

Deem, R. and Salaman, G. (eds) (1985) *Work, Culture and Society*. Milton Keynes: Open University Press.

Department of Social Security (1990) *The Way Ahead: Benefits for Disabled People*. London: Department of Social Security.

Department of Trade and Industry (1990) Remote work units for the disabled, in *Conditions of Work Digest*. London: Department of Trade and Industry.

Dex, S. (1985) *The Sexual Divisions of Work*. Brighton: Wheatsheaf.

Disability, Handicap and Society (1992) *Special Issue: Researching Disability*, 7(2).

Disability Now (1993) Plans put jobs in jeopardy, August: 1–9.

Disability Now (1995a) PACT under fire, October: 1–2.

Disability Now (1995b) Fury over access to work, November: 5.

Disability Now (1996a) Limiting of access to work confirmed, February: 4.

Disability Now (1996b) Access to work being squeezed, March: 1–2.

Driedger, D. (1989) *The Last Civil Rights Movement*. London: Hurst and Co.

Elliot, D. and Elliot, R. (1976) *The Control of Technology*. London: Wykeham.

Employment Department (1989) Review of the organisation and staffing of the Employment Service, July.

Employment Department (1990a) Attitudes, the key to more jobs for the disabled, *Employment Gazette*, August: 380.

Employment Department (1990b) *Evaluation of Special Schemes for People with Disabilities*. London: Employment Department Group.

Employment Department (1990c) Registered disabled people in the public sector, *Employment Gazette*, February: 79–83.

Employment Department (1990d) The employment of people with disabilities: research into policies and practices of employers, *IFF Research*, 55.

Equal Opportunities Review (1990) Equal opportunity horizons 3: Americans with Disabilities Act, September: 28–9.

Esping-Andersen, G. (1990) *The Three Worlds of Welfare Capitalism*. Cambridge: Polity.

Fielding, N.G. and Fielding, J. (1986) *Linking Data*. Beverly Hills, CA: Sage.

Finkelstein, V. (1980) *Attitudes and Disabled People: Issues for Discussion*. World Rehabilitation Monograph No. 5. New York: World Rehabilitation Fund.

Finnegan, R., Salaman, G. and Thompson, K. (eds) (1987) *Information Technology: Social Issues*. Milton Keynes: Open University.

Floyd, M. and North, K. (eds) (1985) Information technology and the employment of disabled people. Conference paper, Anglo-German Foundation, City University, London.

Forester, T. (1989) *Computers in the Human Context: Information Technology, Productivity and People*. Oxford: Blackwell.

Francis, A. (1986) *New Technology at Work*. Oxford: Clarendon Press.

Freeman, C. (1974) *The Economics of Industrial Innovation*. Harmondsworth: Penguin.

Freidson, E. (1986) *Professional Powers: A Study of the Institutionalisation of Formal Knowledge*. Chicago: University of Chicago Press.

French, S. (1988) Experiences of disabled health and caring professionals, *Sociology of Health and Illness*, 10(2): 170–88.

Friedmann, R.F., Gilbert, N. and Sherer, M. (eds) (1987) *Modern Welfare States: A Comparative View of Trends and Prospects*. Brighton: Wheatsheaf.

Gallie, D. (1988) *Employment in Britain*. Oxford: Blackwell.

Gallie, D., Marsh, C. and Vogler, C. (eds) (1994) *Social Change and the Experience of Unemployment*. Oxford: Oxford University Press.

Gamble, A. (1988) *The Free Economy and the Strong State*. Basingstoke: Macmillan.

Gartner, A. and Joe, T. (eds) (1987) *Images of the Disabled: Disabling Images*. New York: Praeger.

Giannini, M.J. (1981) Computing and the handicapped: a promising alliance, *Computing*, 14(1): 1–3.

Gill, C. (1985) *Work, Unemployment and New Technology*. London: Polity.

Gleeson, B. (1991) Notes towards a materialist history of disability. Occasional paper, University of Bristol, Department of Geography.

Glendinning, C. (1991) Losing ground: social policy and disabled people in Great Britain 1980–1990, *Disability, Handicap and Society*, 6(1): 3–19.

Goffman, E. (1968) *Stigma: Notes on the Management of Spoiled Identity*. Harmondsworth: Penguin.

Goodall, J. (1988) Living options for physically disabled adults: a review, *Disability, Handicap and Society*, 3(2): 173–94.

Gooding, C. (1994) *Disabling Laws, Enabling Acts*. London: Pluto Press.

Gorz, A. (1990) *Farewell to the Working Class: An Essay in Post Industrial Socialism*. London: Pluto.

Graham, P., Jordan, A. and Lamb, B. (1990) *An Equal Chance, or No Chance: A Study in Discrimination Against Disabled People in the Labour Market.* London: The Spastics Society.

Gramsci, A. (1971) *Selections from Prison Notebooks.* London: New Left Books.

Gregory, S. and Hartley, G. (1991) *Constructing Deafness.* London: Pinter/Open University.

Hakim, C. (1979) *Occupational Segregation.* Department of Employment Research Papers No. 9. London: Department of Employment.

Hakim, C. (1985) *Employers' Use of Outwork.* Department of Employment Research Papers No. 44. London: Employment Department Group.

Hakim, C. (1987) Trends in the flexible workforce, *Employment Gazette,* November.

Hales, G. (ed.) (1996) *Beyond Disability: Towards an Enabling Society.* London: Sage.

Hall, S. and Jacques, M. (eds) (1983) *The Politics of Thatcherism.* London: Lawrence and Wishart.

Hamnett, C., McDowell, L. and Sarre, P. (1989) *The Changing Social Structure.* Milton Keynes: Open University.

Hanna, W.J. and Rogovsky, B. (1991) Women with disabilities: two handicaps plus, *Disability, Handicap and Society,* 6(1): 49–62.

Harrison, J. (1987) *Severe Physical Disability: Responses to the Challenge of Care.* London: Cassell.

Hawkridge, D. and Vincent, T. (1985) *New Information Technology in the Education of Disabled Children and Adults.* London: Croom Helm.

Hazan, P. (1981) Computing and the handicapped, *Computing,* 14(1): 2.

Heppel, J. (1992) Personal communication.

Hughes, J. (1990) *The Philosophy of Social Research.* London: Longman.

Humphries, S. and Gordon, P. (1992) *Out of Sight: The Experience of Disability 1900–1950.* London: Channel Four Books.

Huws, U. (1984) New technology homeworkers, *Employment Gazette,* January.

Ingstad, B. and Reynolds-Whyte, S. (eds) (1995) *Disability and Culture.* Berkeley: University of California Press.

Jenkins, R. and Solomos, J. (eds) (1987) *Racism and Equal Opportunities Policies in the 1980s.* Cambridge: Cambridge University Press.

Johnson, T. (1972) *Professions and Power.* London: Macmillan.

Jones, V. (1986) *Visually Handicapped Computer Personnel.* London: Royal National Institute for the Blind.

Jowett, S. (1982) *Young Disabled People: Their Further Education, Training and Employment.* Windsor: National Foundation for Educational Research/Nelson.

Karpf, A. (1988) *Doctoring the Media: The Reporting of Health and Medicine.* London: Routledge.

Kaufman, T. and Lincoln, P. (eds) (1991) *High Risk Lives.* Bridport: Prism Press.

Kerr, C. (1962) *Industrialism and Industrial Man.* London: Heinemann.

Kivisto, P. (1981) The theorist as seer: the case of Bell's post industrial society, *Quarterly Journal of Ideology,* 5: 39–43.

Knights, D. and Willmott, H. (eds) (1985) *Job Design: Critical Perspectives on the Labour Process.* London: Gower.

Kuh, D., Lawrence, C., Tripp, J. and Creber, G. (1988) Work and work alternatives for disabled young people, *Disability, Handicap and Society,* 3(1): 3–27.

Kumar, K. (1978) *Prophecy and Progress: The Sociology of Industrial and Post Industrial Societies.* Harmondsworth: Pelican.

Landes, D. (1969) *The Unbound Prometheus: Technological Change and Industrial Development in Western Europe from 1750 to the Present.* Cambridge: Cambridge University Press.

Leclercque, D. and Deghaye, M. (1988) New technology and the handicapped. Conference paper, Congress on New Technology and Disabled People, Liege, Belgium, March.

Lee, G. and Loveridge, R. (eds) (1987) *The Manufacture of Disadvantage*. Milton Keynes: Open University Press.

Leonard, A. (1994) *Right from the Start*. London: The Spastics Society.

Liff, S. (1990) Clerical workers and new technology: gender relations and occupational change, *New Technology, Work and Employment*, Spring: 44–55.

Littler, C. (1982) *The Development of the Labour Process in Capitalist Societies*. London: Heinemann.

Littler, C. (1984) *The Experience of Work*. Aldershot: Gower.

Locker, D. (1983) *Disability and Disadvantage: The Consequences of Chronic Illness*. London: Tavistock.

Loney, M., Boswell, D. and Clarke, J. (eds) (1983) *Social Policy and Social Welfare*. Milton Keynes: Open University Press.

Loney, M., Bocock, R., Clarke, J., Cochrane, A., Graham, P. and Wilson, M. (eds) (1987) *The State or the Market: Politics and Welfare in Contemporary Britain*. London: Sage.

Lonsdale, S. (1986) *Work and Inequality*. London: Longman.

Lonsdale, S. (1990) *Women and Disability: The Experience of Physical Disability Among Women*. London: Macmillan.

Lyon, D. (1988) *The Information Society: Issues and Illusions*. Oxford: Blackwell.

MacDonald, K. (1995) *The Sociology of the Professions*. London: Sage.

MacFarlane, J. (1990) Skills of the disabled: a vital resource, *Information Technology and Public Policy*, 8(3): 178–80.

MacKenzie, D. and Wajcman, J. (eds) (1985) *The Social Shaping of Technology*. Milton Keynes: Open University Press.

Martin, J., Meltzer, H. and Elliot, D. (1988) *OPCS Surveys of Disability in Great Britain, Report No. 1: The Prevalence of Disability Among Adults*. London: HMSO.

Martin, J., White, A. and Meltzer, H. (1989) *OPCS Surveys of Disability in Great Britain, Report No. 4: Disabled Adults: Services, Transport and Employment*. London: HMSO.

Marx, K. (1954) *Das Kapital*. Volume 1. London: Lawrence and Wishart.

Massie, B. (1994) *Disabled People and Social Justice. Evidence to the Commission on Social Justice*. London: Institute for Public Policy Research.

Morris, J. (1989) *Able Lives: Women's Experiences of Paralysis*. London: Women's Press.

Morris, J. (1991) *Pride Against Prejudice: Transforming Attitudes to Disability*. London: Women's Press.

Morris, J. (ed.) (1996) *Encounters with Strangers: Feminism and Disability*. London: Women's Press.

Moses, J.F. (1988) Preparing for a brave new workplace: the impact of new technology on the employment of people with disabilities, *International Rehabilitation Review*, December: 7–10.

Mouffe, C. (ed.) (1979) *Gramsci and Marxist Theory*. London: Routledge and Kegan Paul.

Murray, B. and Kenny, S. (1990) Teleworking as an employment option for people with disabilities, *International Journal of Rehabilitation Research*, 13: 205–14.

Niwa, S. (1988) New technology and the employment of disabled people. Conference paper, Congress on New Technology and Disabled People, Liege, Belgium, March.

Oliver, M. (1990) *The Politics of Disablement*. London: Macmillan.

Oliver, M. (ed.) (1991) *Social Work, Disabled People and Disabling Environments*. London: Jessica Kingsley.

Oliver, M. (1992) Changing the social relations of research productions? *Disability, Handicap and Society*, 7(2): 101–15.

Oliver, M., Zarb, G., Silver, J., Moore, M. and Salisbury, V. (1988) *Walking into Darkness: The Experience of Spinal Injury*. London: Macmillan.

Pahl, R.E. (1984) *Divisions of Labour*. Oxford: Blackwell.

Pennington, S. and Westover, B. (1989) *Hidden Workforce: Homeworkers in England 1850–1985*. Basingstoke: Macmillan.

Perlman, L.G. and Hansen, C.E. (eds) (1989) *Technology and the Employment of Persons with Disabilities*. Switzer Monograph. Alexandria, VA: National Rehabilitation Association.

Pettigrew, A. (1975) Strategic aspects of the management of specialist activity, *Personnel Review*, 4(1): 5–13.

Phillips, A. and Taylor, B. (1980) Sex and skill: notes toward a feminist economics, *Feminist Review*, 6(1): 79–88.

Prescott-Clarke, P. (1990) *Employment and Handicap*. London: Social and Community Planning Research.

Purcell, K., Wood, S., Waton, A. and Allen, S. (eds) (1986) *The Changing Experience of Employment*. Basingstoke: Macmillan.

RADAR (1990a) *Employment and Training for People with Disabilities*. London: RADAR.

RADAR (1990b) Employment and training for people with disabilities: a discussion document, *RADAR Project Newsletter*, 3, September: 3–6.

RADAR (1991) Evaluation of special employment schemes, *Contact*, Summer: 25–6.

RADAR (1993a) Changes in employment support for disabled people, *RADAR Bulletin*, July: 7.

RADAR (1993b) Action needed to save support services, *RADAR Bulletin*, November: 4.

RADAR (1993c) CBI urges government to reconsider changes to support schemes, *RADAR Bulletin*, December: 4.

RADAR (1994) Government concession on access to work scheme, *RADAR Bulletin*, March: 1–2.

Rajan, A. (1985a) *Information Technology and the Disabled Young Workers*. Paris: Organization for Economic Cooperation and Development/Institute of Manpower Studies.

Rajan, A. (1985b) *Training and Recruitment Effects of Technical Change*. London: Institute of Manpower Studies.

Robinson, F. (ed.) (1988) *Post Industrial Tyneside: An Economic and Social Survey of Tyneside in the 1980's*. Newcastle: Newcastle City Libraries.

Rowat, A. (1992) How Germans get jobs, *Disability Now*, October: 11–12.

Royal National Institute for the Blind (1991) *Blind and Partially Sighted Adults in Britain: The RNIB Survey*. London: HMSO.

Sandhu, J. (1987) Information technology and the employment of disabled people, *Employment Gazette*, December: 600–1.

Scherer, M. and Galvin, J.C. (1994) Matching people with technology, *Rehabilitation Management*, 7(2): 128–30.

Schofield, J.M. (1981) *Microcomputer Based Aids for the Disabled*. British Computer Society Monograph. Chichester: Heyden.

Science Policy Research Unit (1982) *Microelectronics and Women's Employment in Britain*. Science Policy Research Unit Occasional Paper No. 17. Brighton: University of Brighton.

Shakespeare, T. (1993) Disabled people's self organisation: a new social movement? *Disability, Handicap and Society*, 8(3): 249–64.

Snowdon Report (1980) *Integrating the Disabled*. London: National Fund for Research into Crippling Diseases.

Soder, M. (1990) Prejudice or ambivalence? Attitudes towards people with disabilities, *Disability, Handicap and Society*, 5(3): 227–41.

Spastics Society (1993) *Wasted Opportunities*. London: Spastics Society.

Spencer, A. and Podmore, D. (1986) *In a Man's World*. London: Tavistock.

Spilsbury, M. (1986) *The Distribution and Growth of the Self-Employed*. Labour Market Studies Mimeograph, University of Leicester.

Stephenson, O. and Parsloe, P. (1993) *Community Care and Empowerment*. York: Joseph Rowntree Foundation and Community Care Report.

Stevenson, J. and Sutton, D.C. (1983) Employment opportunities for physically disabled people in computing in Britain, *International Journal of Rehabilitation Research*, 6(4): 483–5.

Stone, D. (1985) *The Disabled State*. London: Macmillan.

Stonier, T. (1983) *The Wealth of Information*. London: Thames Methuen.

Stubbins, J. (1987) *Towards a National Policy on Vocational Rehabilitation*. World Rehabilitation Monograph. New York: World Rehabilitation Fund.

Swain, J., Finkelstein, V., French, S. and Oliver, M. (1993) *Disabling Barriers, Enabling Environments*. London: Sage/Open University.

Swedish Handicap Institute (1981) *Support for the Disabled in Sweden*. Stockholm: Swedish Handicap Institute.

Swedish Handicap Institute (1992) *Development of Assistive Technology for People with Disabilities*. Vallingby: Swedish Handicap Institute R&D Department.

Taylor, G. and Bishop, J. (eds) (1991) *Being Deaf: The Experience of Deafness*. London: Pinter/Open University.

Taylor, I. (ed.) (1990) *The Social Effects of Free Market Policy*. Hemel Hempstead: Harvester Wheatsheaf.

Taylor, S. and Bogdan, R. (1989) On accepting relationships between people with mental retardation and non-disabled people: towards an understanding of acceptance, *Disability, Handicap and Society*, 4(1): 21–36.

Tenner, E. (1988) The revenge of paper, *The New York Times*, 5 March.

Thomas, A., Bax, M. and Smyth, D. (1989) *The Health and Social Needs of Young Disabled Adults with Physical Disabilities*. Oxford: Blackwell/MacKeith.

Thomas, D. (1982) *The Experience of Handicap*. London: Methuen.

Thompson, E.P. (1967) Time, work discipline and industrial capitalism, *Past and Present*, 38: 56–97.

Thompson, K. (ed.) (1984) *Work, Employment and Unemployment*. Milton Keynes: Open University Press.

Thompson, P. (1983) *The Nature of Work*. London: Macmillan.

Toffler, A. (1980) *The Third Wave*. London: Pan.

Tomlinson Committee (1942) *Report on the Employment of Disabled People*. London: HMSO.

Topliss, E. (1982) *Social Responses to Handicap*. London: Longman.

Turner, R. (1980) The theme of contemporary social movements, *British Journal of Sociology*, 391: 59–73.

United States Civil Service Commission (1947) *Performance of Physically Handicapped Workers*. Washington, DC: US Civil Service Commission.

UPIAS (1976) *Fundamental Principles of Disability*. London: Union of Physically Impaired Against Segregation.

Vandergoot, D. (1987) *Vocational Rehabilitation: Problems and Prospects*. World Rehabilitation Monograph. New York: World Rehabilitation Fund.

Wajcman, J. (1991) *Feminism Confronts Technology*. Oxford: Polity.

Walby, S. (ed.) (1986) *Patriarchy at Work*. Oxford: Polity.

Weinberg, N. (1990) *Computers in the Information Society*. London: Westview Press.

Weiner, C. (1975) The burden of rheumatoid arthritis: tolerating the uncertainty, *Social Science and Medicine*, 9(2): 97–104.

West, J. (1982) *Work, Women and Labour Market*. London: Routledge and Kegan Paul.

Which? (1989) No Entry. October.

Williams, F. (1989) *Social Policy: A Critical Introduction*. Cambridge: Blackwell/Polity.

Witz, A. (1992) *Professions and Patriarchy*. London: Routledge.

Wood, P. (1981) *International Classification of Impairments, Disabilities and Handicaps*. Geneva: World Health Organization.

Wood, S. (ed.) (1982) *The Degradation of Work?* London: Hutchinson.

Wood, S. (ed.) (1989) *The Transformation of Work: Skill Flexibility and the Labour Process*. London: Unwin Hyman.

Wright-Mills, C. (1959) *The Sociological Imagination*. Harmondsworth: Penguin.

Zarb, G. (1992) On the road to Damascus: first steps towards changing the relations of research production, *Disability, Handicap and Society*, 7(2): 125–38.

Zimbalist, A. (ed.) (1979) *Case Studies in the Labour Process*. New York: Monthly Review Press.

Index

STRUGGLES FOR INCLUSIVE EDUCATION
AN ETHNOGRAPHIC STUDY

Anastasia Vlachou

This is a lucid, authoritative and original study of teachers' views and attitudes towards the integration into mainstream schooling of a particular group of children defined as having special educational needs. It offers one of the clearest and most comprehensive analyses of the socio-political mechanisms by which the 'special' are socially constructed and excluded from the normal education system that has so far been produced.

Sally Tomlinson,
Professor of Educational Policy at Goldsmiths College,
University of London

In its detailed analysis of primary school teachers' and pupils' attitudes towards integration, this book locates the question of inclusive education within the wider educational context. The wealth of original interview material sheds new light on the reality of everyday life in an educational setting, and shows us the nature and intensity of the struggles experienced by both teachers and pupils in their efforts to promote more inclusive school practices. The author's sensitive investigation of the relationship between teachers' contradictory views of the 'special' and their integration, and the wider social structures in which teachers work, adds to our understanding of the inevitable difficulties in promoting inclusive educational practices within a system which functions via exclusive mechanisms.

This book will be of interest to students of education, sociology and disability as well as teachers and policy-makers involved in inclusive education. The original methodologies adopted when working with the children will also appeal to students of attitudinal, disability and educational research.

Contents
Preface – Acknowledgements – Introduction – Part 1: Setting the theoretical scene – Disability, normality and special needs: political concepts and controversies – Towards a better understanding of attitudes – Part 2: Teachers' perspectives – Teachers and the changing culture of teaching – Teachers' attitudes towards integration (with reference to pupils with Down's Syndrome) – Part 3: Children's perspectives – Integration: the children's point of view – Disabled children and children's culture – Conclusion – Appendices – Index.

208pp   0 335 19763 9 (Paperback)   0 335 19764 7 (Hardback)

RESEARCHING DISABILITY ISSUES

Michele Moore, Sarah Beazley, June Maelzer

This book is designed to meet a growing need for clear illustrations of how to carry out research which seeks to explore disability issues. It aims to demonstrate the value of a critical attention to social, rather than medical starting points for researching disability, through reviewing a variety of studies which look at different aspects of disabled people's lives. Different quantitative and qualitative methodological frameworks are considered, ranging from analysis of observation data concerning disabled children in schools to rich conversation-based data which focuses on family life. A central theme concerns the pivotal role of disabled people in research. The book provides substantive examples of the dilemmas which face researchers and connects these to ideas for individual personal action. Disabled and non-disabled researchers, professionals and students from a wide range of disciplines will find the presentation of both research findings and debates informative and of interest.

Contents

112pp   0 335 19803 1 (Paperback)   0 335 19804 X (Hardback)

DEAF AND DISABLED, OR DEAFNESS DISABLED?
TOWARDS A HUMAN RIGHTS PERSPECTIVE

Mairian Corker

Deaf people's quest for self-definition and self-determination has tended to take one of two divergent paths, each embracing vastly different and often conflicting conceptualizations of deafness and disability and their relationships to contemporary socio-cultural and political contexts. Because fragmentation works against collective empowerment and effective political challenges to oppression, there is a great need to identify a common discourse which all deaf and disabled people can share without compromising fundamental beliefs and values. This book is the first to use a multidisciplinary, postmodernist approach in the search for an inclusive framework for understanding deafness and disability, which aims to liberate the political potential of socio-cultural diversity and develop our thinking about disability as a form of social oppression. In using this approach, it exposes the essentialism inherent in existing social, political and service frameworks which confuse issues of needs and rights and contribute to the creation and reinforcement of the power imbalances at the heart of disability oppression.

Contents
Acknowledgements – Introduction – First principles – Refocusing – Meaning what we say and saying what we mean – Books without pictures – The power of well-being – Running twice as fast – The time has come . . . – Glossary – References – Index.

176pp   0 335 19699 3 (Paperback)   0 335 19700 0 (Hardback)